CRAP HAPPENS

• • •

Wallowing is Optional

CRAP HAPPENS

•••

Wallowing is Optional

Cindy Keiger

Books

Published 2015 by MarAnKa Books

Cover Design by Katie Russell

Author Photo by Weldon Keiger

ISBN-13: 978-0692556276
ISBN-10: 0692556273

Printed in the United States of America

I lovingly dedicate this book to
Weldon Keiger ♥

TABLE OF CONTENTS

1
INTRODUCTION

The farmer takes a wife, the farmer takes a wife.
Hi-ho, the DAIRY-o, the farmer takes a wife.

~a courtship game from Germany

I married a dairy farmer when I was 53 years old. Hearing my story, people inevitably ask, "Did you ever think you'd end up on a dairy farm?" As if I could imagine something that had never even tiptoed across my mind. Imagining aside, here's a bit of background to acquaint you with the real-life events that brought me here.

My not-yet-husband Weldon and I met via an online dating site. We both lived in North Carolina but, in retrospect, the hundred miles that separated us was nothing compared to the difference in our lifestyles. I had been living the single-again, corporate life in Charlotte for ten years, and Weldon had spent all of his 52 years on the family dairy farm near the small town of King.

As we got to know each other through daily e-mails and chatting on the phone, I was careful to ask the important questions: Is your divorce final? *Yes.* Do you live near water? *Yes, a creek runs through the farm and a river borders one edge of the property.* Would you plant raspberries for me? *Well, there are black raspberries growing on the edge of the yard.* With the essentials out of the way, we began our back-and-forth Saturday or Sunday drives between Charlotte and the farm. He liked me. I liked him.

From the beginning, Weldon made it clear that he wasn't looking for a dairy hand and no way was he expecting me to help with the farm chores. It seemed to be a match made in heaven. Seven months after our initial meeting, we married and I moved from the city to the country.

With my adventurous, can-do attitude, I walked into a world where crap is an everyday event. This new lifestyle seemed unlike anything I had experienced before—marriage, motherhood, life in the woods of northern Minnesota, missionary work in Haiti, eight-to-five office duties. Nope! It seemed I was ill-prepared physically, emotionally, and spiritually for life on a dairy farm. It wasn't long before I started whining (only on the inside, of course) as the daily, unfamiliar grind rubbed me in all the wrong ways.

Using farm vernacular, life is full of crap. According to the dictionary, crap is trash, stuff and nonsense, aggravation, or the real deal: manure. Some people find the "c" word to be vulgar and disgusting, and they are shocked when they hear it being tossed about so nonchalantly. Perhaps I should have put a warning label on this book.

Be it real, proverbial, or psychological, you don't have to live on a farm to experience icky stuff and sticky situations. Frustrations, difficulties, and setbacks happen, but we always have a choice: deal with the yuck or wallow in it. In reading about my struggles and victories, I hope you'll recognize a similarity to problems you are facing and find encouragement to win those battles.

God is using daily life on the farm to work something new in me, making me more real and more thankful. I'm not speaking of a presto-change-o, hocus-pocus magic trick that suddenly turns life into delight upon delight, topped with a dollop of whipped cream. That's not gonna happen. Rather, when life gets challenging or down-right ugly, a change in our perspective can change our attitude, and a change in attitude may be just what's needed to restore our joie de vivre.

Walk with me ... but watch out for the crap.

2

COWS ARE OUT!

Well, humor is the great thing, the saving thing, after all. The minute it crops up, all our hardnesses yield, all our irritations and resentments flit away, and a sunny spirit takes their place.

~Mark Twain[1]

Farmers get up before the first rays of the sun sneak across the fields. Being a morning person, I wasn't intimidated by an alarm clock sounding at five a.m. It was quite pleasant, actually, to have a radio announcer wake us rather than the rude jangling of an alarm. Also pleasing to me was the fact that Weldon doesn't eat breakfast at that early hour. He simply pours himself a glass of juice, has a cookie or a piece of toast, and heads out to chores. I'm left to enjoy a leisurely cup of coffee, read my Bible and daily devotional, and then prepare our breakfast.

Barring any unforeseen occurrences, Weldon returns to the house around 9:00, and I plan accordingly. This morning, the kitchen smells of fried sausage, fresh off the griddle. Maybe I'll make homemade waffles tomorrow, but frozen, store-bought will do today. I put a bowl of dry cereal on the table with a banana snuggled up close.

Ah, here he comes now. He tosses the newspaper on the table, washes up at the kitchen sink, and gives me a smooch. "Good morning, again, sweetie. It sure smells good in here." He puts ice in his glass and fills it with dairy-fresh milk. Very dairy-fresh milk. He sits down and opens the newspaper as I set a plate with his sausage, bun, and hot waffles beside his bowl of cereal. Checking to make sure I haven't forgotten anything, I sit down to my bowl of cold cereal.

Reaching for my hand, he prays, "Lord, thank you for this new day. Thank you that chores went well. Thank you for this breakfast and bless Cindy for preparing it. Bless our families, wherever they be, and keep us on the straight and narrow today. In Jesus' name. Amen."

The kitchen table is situated so Weldon can see out the front window from where he sits. He likes to keep tabs on any activity in the barnyard and along the dirt road that separates our yard from the rest of the farm. I slice a banana over my cereal, pour on the milk, and open my section of the paper to the comics. Ah, the simple pleasure of cool milk, crisp cereal, and velvety smooth banana on my tongue. Weldon makes happy noises while he munches on the waffles and crunches his cold cereal sans milk. He comments on an article in the newspaper, looks up, and exclaims, "Oh, crap! The cows are out!" With that, he's up and out the door.

Wait! My Cheerios will get soggy! But, what's a new wife to do? I slip into my shoes and hurry after him to see what all the hubbub is about. Sure enough, black and white cows are kicking up dust in the road, a few are lazily pulling up grass near the tractor shed, and the others are greedily eyeing the bales of hay in the hay barn.

Weldon circles down the road, herding errant cows back toward the barnyard, while his mom and older sister Pat jog up the road toward us. They live here on the farm and always keep an eye out their kitchen window, too. I guess it's a farm thing. Pat calls to Weldon, "Where do you want to bring them in?"

"Right over there by the big silo," he yells, pointing. "I guess I left the gate open after feeding them this morning."

With that, Pat and Mom Edith spread their arms and shoosh the cows away from the hay barn, toward the open gate. Weldon tells me to round up the hooligans hiding on the back side of the tractor shed. "Spread out your arms and make yourself real big. Don't use your cute little kitty cat voice. Sound mean. Chase them toward the silo, but don't let them hurt you."

Don't let them hurt me? They might hurt me? What in the world had I gotten myself into? But, what's a new wife to do? Coming up behind them, I stretch out my arms as wide as I can and wave frantically. I scared the crap out of two of them. Plop! Splat!

"Eeuuuww. They're crapping on me." That did it. With the deepest, gruffest voice I could summon, I bellowed, "Okay, that's enough! I'm serious, you guys. Get back where you belong!"

They kick up their heels, clods of earth flying, and hurriedly join their cohorts in the mad rush to get back through the gate. Weldon securely fastens the chain behind them, and I heave a sigh of relief.

"Welcome to the farm," Pat calls out, a sly smile on her face.

They went home, we went home, and, yes, my Cheerios were soggy.

Thus ended my first up-close and personal experience with the cows. It didn't take long to learn that this isn't an unusual occurrence on the farm. When a gate is inadvertently left open, cows find it and make their exit. If an electric fence sags, they adopt their best imitation of lithesome deer and attempt to jump over it, milk-heavy udders be damned. Depending on the season and where the darlings have gone, the roundup can be sloppy and slippery, sweaty and dirty, or just plain tiring as we traverse hill and dale in search of the vagabonds and herd them back to the barn.

There's never a convenient time to hear "Cows are out!"

The first time was an interesting, new experience; over the years, it became a disheartening interruption. *Why can't he fix these fences? Doesn't he know how to close the gates?*

It didn't take me long to realize that I don't like cows very much. For one thing, they're awfully big. Cows aren't playful or cuddly, and they pee and poop wherever they want. To top it all off, their big, dark eyes make me feel certain that they're sad, and that makes *me* sad.

But cows don't look sad when they escape their confines and cavort like first-graders at recess. Get two or three or twenty-three of them out in the field (or the front yard—not quite so funny), and I laugh out loud. "Go for it, girls. Enjoy it while you can."

My attitude improved when I saw the escape from the cows' joyous point of view. While rounding up the frolicking delinquents, I now find myself shouting something crazy, like "If you love them, set them free." Once I suggested to Weldon, "Let's call our herd *Cows without Borders* and the neighbors can milk any that wander into their yards. That would be a win/win situation." If I have any breath left while galumphing through the fields, I might even break into a goofy song.

It's a fact of life on the farm: As long as there are cows, they'll find a way out of their fences. A little humor, along with a dash of anthropomorphism, turns the aggravation into a slight bump in the day's road.

But, please, *please* don't call me at two in the morning with a frantic, "Cows are out!" My sense of humor is sound asleep at that hour.

3
WELCOME TO THE FARM

Yet, life within the home was rich and warm. There was no question about one's belonging to a family so close knit and interdependent.

~Patsy Moore Ginns[2]

Transitioning to life on the farm was a fruitful season for me. Transforming Weldon's uncared-for house into a home that evoked a loving and comfortable atmosphere was both a pleasure and a challenge. Wonderfully, before we got married, Weldon had new carpeting and laminate flooring installed throughout the house. It felt like a new beginning, in spite of the fact that almost everything else I had to work with was in the old-and-dilapidated category.

I rummaged through heaps of castoff paraphernalia in each room: childhood books, toys, and clothes belonging to Weldon's three daughters; his own treasures, including umpteen cans and plastic containers of nuts, bolts, screws, and bent nails;

duplicate or unneeded kitchen tools, dinnerware, and appliances; and plenty of miscellany that begged the question, "What in the world am I supposed to do with this?"

From top to bottom, I plowed through the accumulation of a few lifetimes. Well, let me clarify: I have never been in the attic, and I hope to never go there; and the basement is still yucky and scary with years-old stacks of who-knows-what covered in dusty cobwebs. More accurately, I thoroughly cleaned the main level of the house.

The good news is that I like cleaning, because the end result gives me a great sense of accomplishment and joy. Really, it does. (In my former life, my sisters-in-law called me Susie Homemaker, and I wore that title proudly.) It didn't happen overnight, but my efforts turned Weldon's office into *our* office and his bedroom became *our* bedroom. I outfitted a second bedroom with the bed and dresser that came with me from Charlotte and, voila! a guest room. By putting my tiny kitchen table and my grandmother's hutch in the third bedroom, I now had a sewing/craft room. My personal treasures lit up corners, peeked at me from shelves, and smiled from the walls. Slowly but surely, the house was beginning to feel like home.

For the first six months of our married life, I continued my Charlotte job by working remotely from the farm. I went from full-time to part-time, and it was the perfect way to slowly change gears from the city to the country. Not only that, but I had to continue making payments on my house in Charlotte until it sold…which it did, in the self-same month that my Charlotte job ended. God is good!

Getting to know Weldon's parents was a pleasure. His dad Wendell, 85 years old when I joined the family, hadn't done farm work for six or seven years and couldn't easily get around because of osteoarthritis, two knee replacements, loss of hearing, and macular degeneration. But what a character! His eyes crinkled with a devilish gleam when he told a slightly off-color joke, and his interesting and funny stories always made me laugh.

My favorite memory of Dad Wendell is as sweet and clear today as the morning he walked up to the house for a visit.

Weldon and Mom Edith were out doing farm stuff, of course, and I was bustling about the house with morning chores of my own. Surprisingly, a knock at the door! Whom should I see standing there but Wendell—in his pajamas and a light jacket.

I stepped out, gave him a hug, and we got comfortable on the porch swing, talking and laughing like a couple of truant school kids. It was priceless…and short-lived. It wasn't long before Edith came striding purposefully up the driveway. "What are you doing out here? And in your pajamas!" She was aghast. I was amused.

"It's okay. I think he wanted some company and didn't realize he was still in his pajamas. We've been having a lovely time together." Edith was embarrassed, apologizing over and over again, but she was also concerned. Although their house is only 550 feet down the road from us, Dad Wendell shouldn't have walked over on his own. There was always the fear that he might fall and not be able to get back up, and no one would know where he was. I understood her fears, of course, but I was happy and blessed by his visit. He liked me.

Weldon's mom was 77 years young when I first met her. She was, and still is, amazing. She stepped in as Weldon's right-hand man on the farm when his dad could no longer do the work. She helps morning and evening with the milking chores, cares for the young stock, and answers Weldon's every call for assistance. She keeps a large garden, quilts, cooks and bakes up a storm, and cares for her family near and far. From day one, she received me with open arms.

After a year-and-a-half of marriage, I began wondering if I could be of assistance in the milk barn. Every now and then I'd broach the subject with Weldon. "Do you think I'd be able to handle some of the morning or evening chores that your mom does? She does too much, and maybe I could give her a little break."

The day came when Weldon and I agreed that perhaps "now" was as good a time as any for me to try my hand at milking cows. We didn't have a clear plan as to how that would happen, but we'd figure it out.

Returning from town that very afternoon, driving slowly through the barnyard, I saw Edith and Weldon standing in the road, seemingly deep in conversation. I stopped. "Hey. What's going on?" Edith explained that Wendell needed a tracheotomy (because of what would soon prove to be cancer of the vocal cords). She was fretting, not knowing how she could keep doing the farm chores and take good care of Wendell at the same time.

Pat, a retired kindergarten teacher, had moved in with her parents after breaking her knee a few years earlier. She had stayed on to help with her dad's care and to do some of the housework while her mom did farm chores. Now Wendell would need extra care around the clock, and it would take both Edith and Pat to provide that care.

I told Mom about Weldon's and my morning discussion regarding chores and my desire to help. A little weight seemed to slide off her shoulders. The next morning, Edith began teaching me how to milk cows. How's that for perfect timing?

4

AND SO IT BEGINS

I can't do everything, but I can do something. The something I ought to do, I can do. And by the grace of God, I will.

~Edward Everett Hale[3]

eldon had avowed he wasn't looking for a dairy maid, and no one cajoled me into milking cows. Rather, I felt like God was leading me to participate in the actual workings of the farm. The Bible, in Jeremiah 29:11, puts it this way: "'For I know the plans I have for you,'" says the Lord. 'They are plans for good and not for disaster, to give you a future and a hope.'" So here I am, ready to give it my best shot.

To help you better understand my new workplace, a simple description follows.

Our milk barn is a cement block building with two rooms. The first room is the milk tank room, the main feature being the stainless steel tank that holds the milk and keeps it cold. The second room is the milk parlor, where the actual milking of the cows takes place. Traversing the ceiling of both rooms are the pipes that carry the milk from the cows to the tank.

The milk parlor is set up in a herringbone pattern. Both of the two long sides of the room have a door at the back which opens to the holding pen, where the cows wait patiently until it's time to come in. A gate at the front of both sides keeps the ladies in place until they've been milked. Each side has six feed bins attached to the outer wall, and the floor has a grate that does its best to catch the cows' plops and whizzes. The cows stand at a slight angle (thus the term "herringbone milking system") with their heads in the feed bins and their butts supposedly over the grate and toward the center of the room where the unsuspecting laborers work. [Side note: If this has piqued your interest (or totally confused you), head to the library, talk to a local farmer, or go to your computer and search "herringbone milking parlour." These resources will speak more clearly than my words.]

When the back doors are opened, twelve cows jostle their way into the milk parlor, six on each side. Weldon, Edith, and I are in the milk pit, the area between the two long sides where the cows are standing. The floor of the pit is 36 inches below the level where the cows stand. Since I'm only five feet tall, much of the milking process happens at my shoulder level or above. The groans from my weakling arms would soon alert me to their displeasure with this new experiment. But, back to the here-and-now of my story.

When the cows are settled down and calmly munching their feed, Mom Edith switches to teaching mode. "Weldon has washed the udders. Now you take a clean, dry cloth from this bucket and wipe the udder dry—not just the teats, but the entire udder. Next, dip each clean, dry teat with this disinfecting solution and, with another clean cloth, wipe each one dry." Other than being scared that a cow would kick me while my hand and arm were under her, I could almost imagine I was washing the table or dusting the furniture.

"Here's the milker," Edith says, as she lifts it from where it hangs and hands it to me. "Turn this knob to start the suction and then attach the four rubber cups to the four individual teats."

That's easier said than done! I hold the heavy milker in one hand, position it just below the cow's udder, and then, with the other hand, I turn on the suction and attach the cups, one by one. Edith is just as short as I am but definitely stronger and more practiced. She handles the job with ease, and I can only hope that I will soon be equally efficient.

When people ask, "How much milk do you get from a cow?" Weldon answers, "All of it." Oh, this guy is a riot! But the milking machine doesn't stop sucking when a cow doesn't have any more milk to give. How am I to know when a cow is finished? Ah, there's a little glass window in the milker that lets me see if milk is still coming from the udder. If I don't see milk in that window, the cow is done. However, that's not good enough for Weldon. "That cow needs a little more pressure on her back right teat. Pull down slightly on that suction cup so we get all her milk." He certainly knows his cows.

One by one, the six cows on the first side finish milking and, one by one, I turn the suction off and hang the milkers back on the post. "After you dip the teats in this protective solution, you can open the front gate on this side and let these cows out." I did it! Six cows milked and just 30 more to go.

I tackled this thing called "chores" as though it were a job like any other job. In my mind, that meant following a schedule. Chores don't happen on schedule, of course, but morning and evening I'd watch the clock and go back to the house when I had put in my two hours. That was usually long enough to do the milking and a little cleanup. Weldon worked for another hour or two until he finished everything else that needed doing.

There you have the simplified version of milking cows. If that's all there were to the job, it really wouldn't be too bad. I didn't tell you that a cow can wiggle her back end so far away that I have to get on my tippy toes, lean forward under her, and reach all the way into the next county to dip her teats. Cows don't want to come in or don't want to go out. If they get sick, they have to be treated and then have to be milked into a separate bucket. They can be cantankerous and kick off the milker. And let's not even talk about the lovely diarrhea that goes through the herd every spring. Milking machines break down, the electricity goes off, or the milk tank isn't cooling. But, at the moment, I was experiencing the thrill of victory: I can do this!

Less than two years after our wedding, milk chores on the dairy farm is my new part-time job. What an adventure! Seriously, is this not way better than having to get up and go to an office every morning? I could complain about having to change into my barn clothes morning and evening, but wherever one works, it seems we dress for the job and change into different apparel when we get home.

Instead of a long commute through rush hour traffic, I walk or jog down to the barnyard. I don't punch a time clock and I'm not docked for coming in late. I can stroll down to the old smoke house to see if any kitties are hiding in there or take time to ooh and aah over a beautiful sunrise. No one tells me I can't stop and pick a handful of raspberries or take a moment to smell the newly-opened peonies.

Although it begins early and ends a little too late for my tastes, I have quite a few hours in the middle of the day to do whatever I want. You know, like cook, clean, shop, do laundry, and the other hundred tasks that fall to the willing homemaker.

This milkmaid business was off to a good start. I didn't know that my attitude would start to curdle, and my new mantra would become *Oh, crap. It's time for chores.*

5

THE LIFE ROMANTIC

*The word romance, according to the dictionary, means
excitement, adventure, and something extremely real.
Romance should last a lifetime.*

~Billy Graham[4]

People tend to have a romantic image of life on the farm, especially if they've never lived on a farm. Getting back to nature, going green, and sustainable farming are hot topics these days, and I suppose many think I'm living the dream. To me, sustainable farming means trying to sustain a good attitude while living in a nightmare. I'm joking…a little.

One evening I posted a comment on Facebook about walking home from the milk parlor through the rain. Debbie, from her warm, dry, comfortable home in Charlotte, remarked, "That sounds so romantic. You're lucky." Very funny. No matter what the movies portray, at the end of a long day there's nothing romantic about trudging home through the dark and the mud, with drops of water dripping off my nose.

My online dating experiment was undertaken with hopes of finding a man whose life I could share and who would share mine. Visions of excitement and adventure? No, not me! My dreams were all about having a meaningful relationship, a true friendship built on life's struggles and joys. Enter the farmer and the dairy farm. Enter reality.

My first trip to Weldon's place began with lunch in Mt. Airy and then a trip to the top of Pilot Mountain. Next, he introduced me to his family, his dogs, and his neighbor, Les, who was the construction coordinator for the building of the Titanic that was used on the movie set. My head was spinning. If I had any romantic thoughts, they definitely weren't about farming or anything green. The fascination had begun: *Weldon is such a gentleman. What a dear family he has, and a famous neighbor.*

Then we toured the farm. There stood the obligatory barn, its red paint flaked and faded long ago. Other tired buildings held lumber, empty plastic containers, or curious black and white calves. In driving over the acreage, my eyes were dismayed at big piles of junk, broken machinery, and cast-off appliances. Knobby logs and chunks of wood lay helter-skelter in open areas beside the road like remnants from a recent hurricane. My neat-freak tendencies were freaking out. Finally a few sights worthy of Norman Rockwell came into view: an old tobacco shed and smoke house (not that I knew what those monikers meant) and a wonderful log cabin dating back to the 1800s. The knots in my gut started to unwind.

And then Weldon took me to his home. He had built the rambler-style house in the '70s and, unfortunately, it didn't look like anything had been done to it since then. The nondescript paint on the siding was peeling like a bad sunburn, and the rain gutters hung at precarious angles. The inside was dark and dated and cluttered...and that's putting it nicely. Let's just say it was almost a deal-breaker. Reality was pounding on the door as I drove back to Charlotte. Those knots in my gut? Yup, they were back.

• • •

Excuse me. There's a herd of cows meandering down the road. I'm not kidding. I'd better see if I can round them up. I'll be right back.

• • •

Now, where was I? Ah, yes. The life romantic. Living the dream. So much for the romantic farm. Next up: Weldon.

Weldon is kind and good and funny—exactly what I was looking for in a companion. Unbeknownst to even me, I was *expecting* a whole lot more. Dare I say it? I hoped he'd do the manly things, like take out the trash. That's a man's job, right? But, no. The trash is my job. In this idyllic country setting, it's not a simple matter of wheeling a big, plastic garbage bin to the curb. For one thing, our road doesn't have a curb. Instead, every other week or so I fill the car trunk with bags of trash and boxes of recyclables and take it all to the local dump/recycle center.

In my little house in Charlotte, it was up to me to keep things in good repair, or a reasonable facsimile thereof. Having a new husband, I figured I'd never need my hammer and screw drivers again. Wrong. Weldon's time is spent fixing things around the farm, not around the house. Everything I did in Charlotte to care for myself and my home I do here on the farm, and many of those tasks are multiplied by two. So much for expectations.

If a dire situation arose, I know Weldon would come through as my knight in shining armor, as long as he wasn't in the fields or under a piece of machinery or milking those blasted cows. I still have a glimmer of hope that, when he retires, Weldon will take care of the things that need doing around the house, as any knight worth his weight in shining armor would do.

My first husband often said, "Don't expect anything from anyone and you won't be disappointed." That seemed like a crazy or lazy way of looking at life. Now I'm not so sure. Great Expectations. It's a catchy name for a novel, but how does it translate to the real world? I'm still not convinced, but, like a hearty beef stew, perhaps it will be more palatable after a long, slow simmer on the back burner.

Learning to let go of my expectations is an ongoing

process. I will continue to love Weldon just as he is, because he is Weldon. The overwhelming strangeness and difficulties of farm life bring the ugliness of preconceived notions and hopes to the surface. I have to be honest with myself and deal with the yuck.

Why am I talking about expectations when this chapter is supposed to be about the romance of life? I started by saying that people have a romantic view of the farm. That is to say, they have an idealized picture of what living on a farm entails. I said I'm a realist, but my hidden hopes proved me misinformed. I wanted the ideal relationship, a beautiful country home, and my every wish granted by Weldon's heroic love for me. I was expecting the life romantic.

Reality isn't always romantic—not on the farm, not in the office, not on a tropical island. Billy Graham's quote at the beginning of this chapter shows one side of romance. Another definition says that romance lacks basis in fact. Life isn't always excitement and adventure. Actually, it can be downright ugly. Crap happens, so what do we do when our thoughts (and life) get stinky?

Philippians 3:14 tells us to press toward the mark of the high calling of God, and Romans 8:37 says we are more than conquerors. I'm not sure what it means to be *more* than a conqueror, but that's how high God calls us to live. We aren't supposed to let the stuff of life, including its unfulfilled dreams and hopes, disappoint us or defeat us. Being strong and courageous, we rise above the crud. Rising above our regrets and unmet expectations precludes wallowing.

Jack Kerouac admitted, "All of life is a foreign country."[5] This world is nice, but not the real deal—more like a way station of sorts. There's a restlessness in our wandering, a knowing that there must be something more. The perfect place I'm longing for is heaven, even though I can't envision what that really means. Hey! I couldn't even imagine what life on a farm would entail.

Some people think talk of heaven is crazy. "You're delusional. Heaven is known as Pie in the Sky, remember? It's just another way of hoping for the life romantic." But I choose to believe the promises of God. One reality is the harsh world all around us, but another reality awaits.

Billy Graham says that romance is extremely real and will last a lifetime. In fact, our romance with God will last beyond this lifetime, on and on, forever. Some day I will wake up brand new in "the life romantic" on the other side.

6

THE BLAME GAME

When we stop to evaluate things, we realize that the thing we're frustrated about is not really the issue. The real problem is with our perspective – it needs adjusting.

~Kay Arthur and Pete De Lacy[6]

I'm gonna wash dishes now," I say, pushing myself away from the breakfast table.

"No, *I'm* gonna wash the dishes this morning," Weldon exclaims.

"No," I reply, standing at the sink. "I can do them."

"I'll flip you for it," and he grabs me and tosses me over his shoulder like a sack of grain.

"Okay, okay," I laugh. "You win." He puts my feet back on the floor and I step away from the sink.

Not long after this little episode, I started complaining of a backache. "Oh, no. I broke your back," lamented Weldon.

"No, you didn't break my back. It's just tired and sore."

For many months afterward, whenever I complained of my back hurting, Weldon would make that same statement: "Oh, no. I broke your back," and each time I would reply, "No, you *didn't* break my back." Thankfully, he finally gave it up.

In this silly example, Weldon was blaming himself for something that wasn't his fault. Not quite as humorous was the way I started blaming the farm for everything that wasn't just right in my life.

Remember, I came to the farm when I was 53 years old. It's quite normal for things to start changing in one's body at that age, but I would have none of that *normal* stuff. No, indeed. It was all the big, bad farm's fault.

Before moving to the farm, I always slept on my side. Always. Some time after settling into my new surroundings, there were many months when a strange pain made it impossible for me to lie on my side. I had never slept on my back before, but the ache in my hips forced me to learn how to sleep in this new position. My mom said she went through the same experience with her hips, but that wasn't good enough for me. "Farm living. This is ridiculous." Fortunately, months and months later, the night finally arrived when I could lie on my hips again. Now I'm able to sleep on either side or my back, so I can toss and turn to my heart's content.

Speaking of my back, when I was younger I thought it was the best part of my body. I remember looking at bathing suits, always choosing one that displayed my back to good advantage. This is no longer the case. First, being older, I'm not wild about choosing *any* bathing suit. Second, since coming to the farm, little bumps occasionally pop up on my back for no apparent reason. They aren't bug bites and when I asked my doctor about them, she said it didn't appear to be a rash and was nothing to worry about. Okay, I don't worry about it, but whatever it is, it's aggravating. When I have an itch, I naturally reach around to scratch it and, in so doing, scratch off a bump. "Oh, crap! Now I'm bleeding!"

Hay fever and allergies had never plagued me, and I always thanked God for that blessing. However (you guessed it), since living on the farm, I cough and complain of a stuffy head way too often. Wouldn't you know, I read that it's not uncommon for allergies and sinus crud to become more prevalent as one gets older. Not only was I getting older, but the farm had introduced a whole new world of junk to my system—various grasses and pollen, cows and cats. I shouldn't have been surprised that my body had to adjust to its new habitat, but I blamed the farm. "Grrr. This lousy farm. Now I have allergies? Sheeesh."

My shins are always black and blue from these stupid work boots. This farm has turned me into a scrooge.

Why do I bother trying to keep the house clean? I might as well let it fall into ruin along with all the other dilapidated buildings.

One of my favorite sayings from Haiti just popped into my head: *Se pa fot mwen.* Interpretation: *It's not my fault.* Drop an egg on the floor and the acceptable response is, "It's not my fault. If the floor weren't so hard, the egg wouldn't have broken." Had this Haitian phrase slyly settled into my heart? Ha! Blame Haiti. Blame the floor. Blame the farm. Blame the rain, the snow. Blame your boss, your husband or wife or kids.

You're probably beginning to get my drift...and I was beginning to drift into a lousy state of mind, not recognizing how skewed my perspective had become. I've read that we're naturally conditioned to have a bias for the negative. I don't know if it's true, but my bias was definitely bending me out of shape.

Luke 6:27 in *The Message* (a contemporary version of the Bible) says, "Love your enemies. Let them bring out the best in you, not the worst." Light bulb moment: I'm seeing the farm as my enemy. I'm making it the scapegoat for my bad attitude. I'm blaming the farm for being a farm.

How can I let the farm bring out the best in me, rather than the worst? I picture my dilemma as being a coin with two sides. First, there's the blame side. To *blame* means to find fault or to hold someone or something responsible. From the examples recounted above, I'd say I've mastered the blame side.

On the flip side of the coin, there's acceptance. To *accept* is to receive willingly, to endure without protest or reaction, or to make a favorable response. Youch! That's pretty painful.

Acceptance. This side of the coin has proved more difficult. Accept the fact that the farm is messy and I'm getting older? Change my perspective so that I respond favorably to growing old on the farm? Actually express approval of the farm and speak nicely about it? I've got my work cut out for me.

Blame is not an option. I don't toss a coin to see if I should cast blame or respond favorably in any given situation. I'm imagining the coin affixed to my forehead with the acceptance side showing. Silly, I know, but it's a start.

Whatever comes, I determine to be and do my best through it all. I'm grumpy? I recognize my grumpiness without blaming it on anyone or anything. Chores are getting me down? There's no sense in blaming the cows. I'll do my chores and do them well, knowing the cows will feel better when they're relieved of all that milk. A pigeon craps on my head? Yes, a pigeon actually crapped on my head when I was feeding a calf last night. No problem. Actually, I saw it as a problem while Pat laughed. When she was done snickering, she told me that some people view this event as good luck, so, after the fact, I tried to see it as a blessing. Key word: tried.

The blame game. Don't play it. There are no winners. Adjusting my perspective to find what is acceptable or even praiseworthy in the yuckiest situations isn't always easy, but it's always worth it.

7

DO WHAT??

One of the greatest discoveries a man makes,
one of his great surprises,
is to find he can do what he was afraid he couldn't do.

~Henry Ford[7]

B ig, powerful equipment scares me. Farm machines are big; I'm small. Even so-called hand-held farm tools are too heavy for me to manage with confidence. I remember the first time Weldon asked me to help him at the silo. The silage wasn't unloading properly from the silo to the feeding trough, and he needed some assistance. "Uhm, okay. What am I going to do?" I asked as I exchanged my flip flops for boots. Weldon's purposeful strides, followed by my hesitant steps, brought us to the silo.

Silos are the tall, concrete cylinders that hold the chopped corn (silage) which the cows eat year-round. Of the three on our farm, ranging in height from 40 to 50 feet, only two are still in use. They stand proud and imposing, their domed tops tickling the clouds.

First, Weldon attached a huge drill to a gear shift on the outside of the silo. He explained that the drill would turn the gear that would raise the unloader inside the silo. "Here, give it a try. Just hold the drill steady and pull this trigger." I have my own drill, and I understand how they work, but this one was at least three times bigger than mine. With feet firmly planted, body leaning in, and both hands grasping the drill, I pulled the trigger. The drill was strong and up to its task, but the weight on the other end of it caused the drill to shudder.

I hung onto that drill as though it might fall to the ground and mash my toes like ten fingerling potatoes, so Weldon found a length of lumber to support and steady both the heavy drill and my quivering nerves. Round two. Feet planted, body leaning, heart palpitating, I pull the trigger. Ah, this is much better. "Okay, I think I can do it."

Weldon continued, "I'm going to climb up the outside of the silo by way of these rungs and get inside to see what's wrong with the unloader. When I get up there, I'll yell down to you to start the drill. When the unloader is raised high enough, I'll shout, 'Stop!'"

"Are you sure I'll be able to hear you above the noise?" He assured me that I would.

"Then," he added, "after I find and fix the problem, you have to flip this switch to reverse the direction of the drill, and the unloader will be lowered back down to the level of the silage." I tried the forward and reverse switches another time or two.

I'm feeling somewhat confident that I can manage the starting and stopping of the drill, but my head is filling with stories Weldon told me about farmers who died from inhaling silo gas. Without going into detail (because I didn't know the "finer" aspects of nitrogen dioxide at the time), all I knew was that silo gas can kill you. A nasty little ball of panic began to swell in the pit of my stomach.

Are you going to be okay up there? Be careful! Yell down

to me every now and then. Don't stay up there too long.

Everything went just fine. I worked the drill, I could hear his commands, and the silo gas didn't kill him. I've done this same task many times over the years, but, until I see Weldon emerging from the silo, the heebie-jeebies always play their game of tag up and down my spine.

Farm vehicles are really big and really far outside my comfort zone. My first experience with a tractor was simply riding with Weldon as he gave me the grand tour of the farm on one of our first dates. One giant step and two normal steps, and I'm on the tractor. I carefully positioned my rear on the fender (which Weldon had graciously attempted to wipe clean). One hand held the edge of the fender and the other clutched the armrest of the tractor seat. *Where's my seat belt?* The fact that a tractor weighs 13,000 pounds didn't make me feel any better about the whole thing. Let me also explain that, like everything else on the farm, Weldon's tractors are old: no cabs, no air-conditioning, windshields, radios, or luxury. Nope. You're just right out there, six feet above the ground, at the mercy of Mother Nature. But six feet above is better than six feet under. I always try to look on the bright side.

With hair whipping in all directions, I breathed deeply (remember, love was in the air), and I was awed by the gorgeous vistas from that height. However, I freaked out when we traversed the side of the first hill and the tractor leaned at a crazy angle. Oh, yes, it leaned sideways till I was certain the tractor would roll over, killing us both in the process. White-knuckled, hanging on for dear life, I pictured tomorrow's headlines in the *Winston-Salem Journal*: "Engaged Couple Killed in Freak Tractor Accident." We survived.

The day came, sure as shootin', when Weldon called through the door, "I need to have both tractors down near the river. Can you come help me?"

"What, you want me to drive a tractor? I can't drive a tractor."

"Sure you can. I'll teach you."

He explained the controls, and I practiced putting it in

and out of gear before we cranked the engine. Then he gave me more instructions: Turn on the key, push the starter button, push in the clutch and the brake, one foot on each.

"Wait a sec. I can't reach them!"

"Sure you can. Scoot to the front edge of the seat and you can do it." Easy for him to say. "Next, take the transmission out of park, shift the lever from neutral into first gear, and slowly release the clutch and brakes." I can drive a straight stick car, so this shouldn't have been difficult. However, multiple levers and each gear having four speeds addled my brain ever so slightly.

Bottom line? With my bottom line barely resting on the seat, I was able to drive the tractor that day. I've done it quite a few times since then, but Weldon always has to remind me of the steps—from jerky takeoff to timid, rumbling arrival at the fields. On the few short straightaways on the gravel road, I actually get going fast enough for the wind to ruffle my hair. Woohoo!

Traversing the fields in the skid loader, roaring high above the ground atop one of the big old tractors, or racing down the road on the four-wheeler (Weldon's newest concession to getting older) would make a hardier soul hoot and holler in pure joy. Me? I'm worried about endangering my life in such blatant manner.

Sophie Tunnell[8] said, "Fear is a slinking cat I find beneath the lilacs of my mind." If I didn't let that sly scaredy-cat in, surely I could drive the tractor with confidence and bravely tackle other jobs so I would be of more help on the farm. Therein lies the problem: I don't *want* to be more helpful on the farm. A woman's place is in the home, not in the fields. That's my story and I'm sticking to it.

8

LIGHTEN UP

Even if there is nothing to laugh about, laugh on credit.

~Anonymous

When a squirrel darts in front of the car while we're out for a drive, Weldon always blurts out a particular exclamation. Always. We were heading into town last week, and I noticed a little squirrel just ahead on my side of the road. For once, I beat him to it: "Run for your life, little guy. Save your balls." Skepticism snorted at me from Weldon's side of the car, and I immediately realized my mistake. "Oops. I mean *Save your nuts.*" Sadly, I never have been able to tell a joke.

Weldon is the comedian in this family. One of the first things that endeared him to me was his ability to laugh and to make me laugh. He can tell a joke, he has crazy stories from his childhood that he loves to recount, his quick comebacks are right on target, and he is quite the actor.

Milking cows, however, is serious business, especially with

all that crap flying around. Yet Weldon and I have some of our best interactive moments while working in that smelly milk pit. Chore time is as close to "date night" as we get, so we make the most of it.

My favorite times, morning or evening, are when one or the other of us bursts into song. The melody is always a familiar tune, but the words are made up on the fly and, almost always, relate to cows.

"I see a cow tail rising. I think the crap is going to fly. Oh, don't come around tonight, it'll hit you in the eye. There's a cow tail on the rise."

And another golden oldie: "Make the poop go away, and get it off my shoulder. Oh, I think it's in my hair. Please don't make me leave it there."

On the farm, we take our humor wherever we find it. I recently read a little funny about dusting. (Remember, dusting is serious business in my world.) It said something like *Don't worry if your furniture is dusty. Use it as an opportunity to leave a little message for your sweetie.* Ha! I knew how that would turn out, but I decided to give it a try. Dragging my finger through the thick layer of dust atop the little red cabinet in the front room, I scrawled, *Hi, Weldon. I love you.* I sealed my sweet message with the flourish of a beautiful heart. Weldon didn't see the message—not that day, not the next day. Since he doesn't see dust, I wasn't surprised that he didn't notice a message in the dust.

Despite my love of smiles and laughter, I live by numerous self-imposed rules which suck the joy out of life. These rules beat me up every day on the farm. Piles of junk wherever I look, broken equipment making daily chores more difficult, calves born at inopportune moments, and cows sneaking out of their confines all work against my innate sense of what's proper and orderly.

Unfortunately, I have just as many complaints about how things are done and not done inside the house. Why are there outlets that don't work and wires hanging out of holes in the walls and ceiling? Will the window casings ever be finished? A man's home is his castle, but it's obvious that Weldon's idea of a castle and mine come from two different fairy tales.

I'm guilty of quite a few unfinished projects of my own. Here the start of a quilt, there a pile of mending. Hooks waiting to be hung behind the bedroom door, pictures longing to be added to the family photo wall. A basement beyond scary in its unruliness, an attic …. Stop! Nightmarish horrors lurking in the attic are not allowed in my head.

To be clear, I don't care how disheveled *your* environment is, but I prefer *my* space to be relatively neat and tidy. When I walk into the house and find things left lying any old place and see too many tasks undone, my mood goes south pretty quickly. Can our home be just as welcoming when the floors are dirty and the desks are piled high with papers and paraphernalia that haven't found their proper place yet? Weldon certainly thinks so. Perhaps I could adopt his laid-back ways, but then I remember we are two different people, and it's okay.

I'm a stickler for the rules, even if they're my own rules.

- Be on-time or even a few minutes early. Unfortunately, this rule hasn't fared very well since I moved to the farm. My major gripe is Sunday morning. Church starts at 9:30. It would be nice to get there before Connie starts playing the piano so I wouldn't have to hear the greeter's words, "Weldon and Cindy are here. We can start now."

- Clean up after yourself. This includes putting stuff back where it belongs, wiping up spills, putting dirty clothes in the hamper, and other similar little duties.

- Put a new roll of toilet paper on the holder when you use the last of it.

I could go on and on. My rules seem simple enough. I just want a neat and orderly environment. Surely I can expect Weldon to live according to my high standards. Don't all men bow lovingly and obediently to the wife's household regulations?

A quote from Oswald Chambers[9] says, "One of the most cruel ways of killing natural love is by disdain built on natural affinities." Could clinging to my natural bent toward cleanliness, along with criticism of the general yuck of life on the farm, kill my love for Weldon? That's scary enough for me to step back and reconsider what's important.

Weldon has been Weldon for almost 60 years; I don't think he'll start making drastic changes anytime soon. I'd be frowning if he tried to change *me* and the way *I* do things. When it comes to self-imposed rules and regulations, we're going to have to give each other the freedom to be ourselves. Yes, frustration is another option but, trust me, it's a bad one.

We need more parties and dancing, laughter and silliness - even if we have to make it up as we go along. The Preacher, in Ecclesiastes 8:15 (NLT), says it succinctly: "So I recommend having fun, because there is nothing better for people in this world than to eat, drink, and enjoy life. That way they will experience some happiness along with all the hard work God gives them under the sun." Sounds like the Preacher was familiar with farming.

Here are a few good rules we can all live by—rules that will make the home, school, workplace, and world a nicer place: Encourage others. Be kind. Dance. Be thankful. Smile. Pray. Sing. Give a hug. Listen.

Uptight, stickler-for-my-rules me versus spontaneous, happy-go-lucky me is an ongoing battle. I shake my fist at myself and say, "Lighten up!" Really, I do. Since I prefer a glad heart and happy surroundings, my prayer is that the Lord will help me be more carefree and actually follow the little rules I noted in the preceding paragraph. Instead of rigid, I want to be relaxed. I want to laugh more.

Ah. Weldon is in from chores. Maybe he'll have a funny story to tell me while we eat our breakfast.

9

DON'T FENCE ME IN

You hem me in behind and before, and you lay your hand [of protection] upon me.

~Psalm 139:5 (NIV)

One of the first things I learned after moving to the farm was that when cows escape their prescribed confines, they're as giddy as teenagers on spring break. I'm just thankful our party animals don't head to Florida in search of a good time. Should they decide to mosey on down the highway, they and we could be in serious trouble. Cows don't seem to understand that fences are erected for their own good.

Some years ago, Weldon was cutting corn in the fields down by the river, so I was surprised when I heard the tractor pull into the driveway. He came in, explaining rather huffily, "The neighbor's darn horses are in the field. I have to call him before they do any serious damage to the corn."

Until then, it was always our cows that were out, so I

secretly chuckled. "Don't be too hard on him, sweetie. There's probably just a fence down or a gate left open." I was so wise, had so much experience with farm happenings.

It's not only cows and horses that long to stretch their boundaries and try new things. Just the other day, I watched a kitten climb higher and higher into a tree, perhaps to feel the wind in her fur or to discover what was on the other end of that big Lincoln Log. But then there she sat, mmrowing sorrowfully with no idea how she got into such a predicament. Refusing to call the fire department, I cajoled and wheedled until, one hesitant paw placement after another, she clawed her way back to terra firma.

During one of my grandson Marshall's first visits to the farm, I told him he could explore till the cows came home, "But don't be messing with things you're not familiar with. Stuff around here could be dangerous or harmful to a little guy." After an hour of checking out all the buildings and whacking everything in sight with his magical stick-turned-sword, he came to the house looking like a guilty Smurf. He had gotten into a container of carpenter's chalk, and he was unsuccessful in brushing the residue from his hands, face, and clothes. He had been stretching the boundaries, for sure.

After being single-again for many years, I guess you could say I was feeling adventurous when I decided to try online dating. Who knew where this bold new "stretching" might lead? It was both scary and exciting as I pushed against my introverted tendencies. If someone had told me I'd be living and working on a dairy farm within a couple of years, I would have laughed, slapped my knee, and said, "That's a good one!"

But here I am, with a whole new set of fences surrounding my life. The strangeness of the daily routines closes in on me until I want to scream or run away. Since I'm not good at doing either of those, I just get gloomy.

Enter Weldon's sister Pat. From the beginning, knowing I might miss city life, she became my social director. She takes me to museums, gardens, and local shops; to plays and art galleries; to historic locations and the best book stores around. I don't know what I would do without her.

When I'm longing for a broken fence post or an open gate to sneak through, Pat often comes to the rescue. "I'm making a run to Winston today. Do you want to ride along?" I have no idea where we're going, and I don't care. She knows all the roads, the best coffee shops, and the newest sweet-treat locations. We always roll back into the farm grinning like Cheshire cats, with just enough time for me to throw some supper on the table for Weldon.

When a few hours away aren't enough to cure the malaise, I have the freedom to spend a weekend in Charlotte with Anna and Marshall. The combination of no cows, no cats, no alarm clock, and no cooking lets me return home refreshed in body and soul.

Weldon doesn't feel fenced-in on the farm. It's always been his home, his family is here, and he loves his work. Of course he gets tired and frustrated now and then, but he isn't like the cows and me, who are gazing longingly at those greener pastures, just over yonder. He keeps doing what needs doing and then does some more. He's amazing!

Look at the following verse from Psalm 139:5 (NASB). "You (God) have enclosed me behind and before, and laid Your hand upon me." Instead of the word *enclosed*, other versions say encircled, squeezed, or hedged in. What? God has fenced me in? It almost sounds like I'm in a trap, and being in a trap doesn't elicit joyous hymns of elation.

However, the New International Version puts it like this: "You *hem me in* behind and before, and you lay your hand upon me." Hem. I know what it means to hem. In sewing, I hem the edges to keep them from fraying, especially with fabric that is more delicate and fragile. God keeps his hand on me in a protective manner, hemming me in so I don't unravel or come undone. Ahh, a blessing in disguise.

Fences are a means of security and protection. Fences keep our animals in where they belong and, at the same time, keep other animals and dangers out. We, as humans, have boundaries, as well. They can be physical, keeping us from physical harm, or they can be internal (mental or spiritual), allowing us to live safely and peacefully with ourselves and others.

For the Children's Message in church one Sunday, I told the kids that Jesus is like a mother hen. Everyone laughed, but it's a good picture of the security we have as Christians. Luke 13:34 says, in part, "How often I have wanted to gather your children together as a hen protects her chicks beneath her wings...." A mother hen isn't being mean when she gathers her babies around her. She's offering warmth and protection and love. Mom is a fence for her little ones, but the chicks are probably squawking *Let me go! Let me go!*

Along the same lines, God wasn't being mean when he moved me to the farm. It's only when my thoughts run amok (outside their prescribed boundaries) that I feel trapped and I scream *Get me outta here. I can't take it anymore!* This is all internal, of course, but still quite pitiful. An old hymn says, "Open my eyes, that I may see glimpses of truth You have for me; place in my hands the wonderful key that shall unclasp and set me free."[10]

Instead of feeling trapped, I recognize that I'm living in a place of freedom and safety. I'm free to bake cookies, take a walk, or work on a crossword puzzle. I can mentally escape by reading, writing, or goofing off on the computer. Life is much better when I remember God's love hems me in and, at the same time, sets me free.

Having said all that, I'm definitely sensing a cup of coffee and a doughnut in my near future. I think I'll give Pat a call.

10

WHO'S IN CHARGE HERE?

While we may not be able to control all that happens to us, we can control what happens inside us.

~Benjamin Franklin[11]

L ook at that sweet girl in her ruffly red dress, all sugar and spice and everything nice, stamping her foot and exclaiming, "You're not the boss of me!" Yes, that little darling still makes an occasional guest appearance in my head.

I remember when a new praise song was introduced that included the words, "It's not about me, as if you [God] should do things my way." I was stunned. It's not all about me? I would never say it out loud, but I pictured God spending a lot of time making sure I was happy. But, taking the words of the song to heart, I tried to see the bigger picture of life centered around God and his plans. Ah, another lesson under my belt.

Not quite. I still get a secret thrill to hear Burger King encouraging me to have it my way. I imagine ruling over my little corner of the world like a queen over her realm. *Shape up, all you peons. From now on, we're doing it my way.*

On the farm, everything revolves around the farmer. Everything. Not even the clock can boss Weldon around. I came up with an ingenious tactic, subconsciously thinking, "You're not the boss of me." Here's my plan: *This is Weldon's farm, his job. I'm not getting up until he does.* Thus, the radio comes on, Weldon turns it off, rolls over, and goes back to sleep. I lie in bed, feigning sleep until he decides to crawl out.

We rise and shine and get the morning going. Right in the middle of my leisurely devotional time, I hear Weldon's parting words, "I'm heading out to chores." That means quiet time is over, I need to prepare the cat food, and get to my duties in the milk parlor. I had sabotaged myself. Why, oh why didn't I get up when the nice man on the radio woke me? Lying in bed until Weldon got up was a silly (stupid?) lesson in aggravation, and he wasn't even aware that I was trying to prove a point.

Mealtimes on the farm must be flexible according to what Weldon is doing. If he's in the middle of harvesting corn, fixing machinery, or walking the fence lines, he can't stop just because it's supper time. For the first couple of years, having supper ready made me want to pull out my hair. I'm a good cook, so that wasn't the aggravation. How do I have everything ready at the same time, especially when I don't know what that "same time" might be on any given day? "It's me, sweetie," he calls as he comes in the door. That's my cue to get supper on the table, regardless of the time.

I finally took a lesson from Mom Edith. She cooks during the day and then uses the microwave to warm the food when it's time to eat. I still cringe a little when I have to do this, however. It seems degrading for today's freshly-prepared main course to be thrown, like yesterday's leftovers, into the microwave.

When Weldon needs an extra pair of hands outside, he calls on me for assistance. Being new to the farm, most of the things he asks me to do are things I've never done before, so I know who'll be the boss when I respond to his call. Darn, I hate that.

The day came when Weldon decided I should learn to drive the skid loader. "If you'll drive the Bobcat, I can walk the fields, pull the weeds, and toss them into the skid loader bucket without having to climb in and out of the machine every few feet."

"But, I can't drive that thing."

"Not yet, but I'll teach you." I think he inwardly chuckles every time he makes that statement. In this instance, after just a few minutes of instruction, I saw it wasn't too difficult. Push both levers forward and it goes forward, pull them back and we're going back. Move just one lever or the other, and I'm turning. Actually, it was fun, but don't tell Weldon I said that.

Now imagine the first time I had to drive the skid loader in what was, to me, a serious situation. A newborn calf had to be transported to the calf shed. Weldon gave me a choice: stand in the bucket and keep the calf from squirming out as Weldon drove, or drive the skid loader and let Weldon hang onto the calf. Since the calf was almost as big as I, I decided to drive.

I climb into the cab, settle into the seat, pull down the safety bar till it locks into place, and position my feet on the pedals. Weldon walks me through the process, step by step. "Turn on the key, press the little button up near the roof, put your hands on the two levers and push them forward to go forward, pull them back to back up." Okay, I've done this much before and I can do it again.

"Now, raise the bucket. The heel of your left foot raises the bucket; the toe of your left foot lowers the bucket. The heel of your right foot turns the bucket up, keeping the contents in place; the toe of your right foot dumps the contents out." Practicing each step a few more times, Weldon thinks I'm ready. My quivering innards aren't convinced.

While driving to pick up the calf, Weldon is encouraging me from his position in the bucket and reminding me of each step. When we get to the calf, he jumps out, lifts the calf into the bucket, plants his feet firmly on either side of it, and continues to give me instructions. And, we're off. When Weldon does it, it's smooth as glass, just so, quick as a wink. And when I do it? Chop.

Jerk. Oops. Groan. I was afraid I'd dump farmer and calf on their heads and then, unwittingly, run over them both. We all arrived safely at the shed, although I was a nervous wreck when we got there.

I would be tickled pink if I could control chore time. This is how things would occur. Weldon starts the silo unloader and it runs smoothly, with nary a hitch. The cows walk placidly into the holding pen, no cajoling necessary. The calves are waiting patiently. They don't butt the bottles out of our hands, and all are healthy and happy. In the milk parlor, every machine runs as it should, the electricity doesn't go out, and no one comes to chat or borrow a tool. The cows don't kick, pee, or poop. The farm is running like a well-oiled machine, and we are back to the house in record time.

Yes, I dream of being the boss. Unfortunately, life just happens all around me (the good, the bad, and the downright ugly), taking no regard of my lofty plans to rule the world.

Near the beginning of this chapter, I noted that everything on the farm revolves around Weldon. You saw the fallacy of that right off, didn't you? Even he can't control the cows, the fences, the breakdowns, or the weather. He has to deal with whatever life throws at him, and he almost always does it with aplomb. He inspires me.

Ultimately, life is not about *me* and doing things my way, but about *we* and working together. Life is a communal experience, and our longing for power and control is divisive and, in the final analysis, a pipe dream. Ephesians 4:16 shows us a better way. "He (God) makes the whole body fit together perfectly. As each part does its own special work, it helps the other parts grow, so that the whole body is healthy and growing and full of love."

We each have an area of expertise, yet we need one another to experience the fullness of life. When I'm weak, someone can be strong for me. When I'm doing what I'm good at, others can learn from me. That sweet girl in her ruffly dress just needed a little human interaction. And maybe a swat on the butt.

"As each part does its own special work, it helps the other parts grow." I'm learning the truth of this on the farm. In spite of my grumblings and groanings, I'm seeing that this is exactly where I need to be. It can be painful, but look at the results: "healthy and growing and full of love." I couldn't ask for more.

11

LITTLE BOXES

If you let go a little, you will have a little peace. If you let go a lot, you will have a lot of peace. If you let go completely, you will have complete peace.

~Ajahn Chah[12]

Dust from gravel roads settles on everything in sight. Grease from machinery slip-slides its way onto hard-working hands and clothes. Chaff and sawdust lodge in any available nook or cranny. Mud, and worse, clings to boots. Need I say more? Life is messy, especially on a farm. When you come to visit, you'll probably end up with crud on your shoes and hay bits or cobwebs in your hair. You might even get crap on the back of your pants, so be careful where you sit, please.

Working alongside Weldon in the milk parlor was vital to making the adjustment to my new habitat. I now understand his long hours, frustrations, dirty clothes, and crusty boots. I understand, but that doesn't mean I accept them with open heart and arms. I'm always trying to find ways to keep the outside world outside, where it belongs.

Weldon clomp clomp clomps to the kitchen sink to wash up. This isn't a gentle washing of hands—but hands, arms, elbows, and, in hot weather, even his face and the back of his neck. Water splish-splashes the floor and the clean dishes drying in the other side of the sink, which I neglected to cover with a dish towel.

Our future laundry room is supposed to solve this aggravation, providing another entrance to the house and a nice big farm sink for his washing-up pleasure. To date, that room exists only in my dreams.

In the face of this ongoing frustration, I decided to take the direct route. "Sweetheart, it would be such a help to me if you'd wash up in the bathroom. You previously explained that the bathroom is further away from the water heater, thereby using more water while waiting for it to get warm. But you could install one of those in-line water heaters. To help cover the expense, I'll contribute $25 a month." He laughed.

I doggedly continued. "There are plenty of hand towels, so you'll always have a clean, dry towel and it will save the kitchen towels from being wet and icky all the time." Lo and behold, he agreed! Weldon said he likes to see me happy. And I *was* happy.

He started well, although he never installed the in-line water heater. If he found himself standing at the kitchen sink, ready to turn on the tap, he'd do an about-face and head down the hallway. Other times, grabbing the kitchen towel with water dripping off his elbows, he'd mumble, "Sorry," like a child caught with his hand in the cookie jar.

After a month or two, it seemed like he gave up, and I did the same. The morning he stood sheepishly washing at the sink, I said, "Just do whatever makes you happy. I'll deal with it." I'm not much for battles, and this didn't seem worth the effort.

My life in Charlotte was tidily compartmentalized. Work followed a set schedule, and home life, with no husband or kids, was orderly. When I cleaned the house, it stayed clean for a long time. If anything was out of place, I was the one who left it there and, sooner or later, I'd put it back where it belonged. This little neat-freak was pretty pleased with herself.

In the not-so-distant past, when I went to visit either of my daughters, I not only washed the dishes we dirtied while preparing and eating a meal, but also scoured the sink and stove and maybe wiped down the fronts of the cabinets. I don't do that anymore. Yes, I wash dishes and wipe up spills that have occurred in the cooking process, but I'm trying to keep this obsession to myself. Actually, I'm trying to get rid of it. Period.

The farm isn't a tidy place. It's a working farm, and you'll never see it featured on the cover of *Farm Beautiful*. (I did quite a few online searches, but couldn't find such a magazine, so don't worry about submitting a subscription form.) Without success, I've tried to teach Weldon the maxim, "A place for everything and everything in its place." He can patch and jerry-rig and make do with the best of them, but keeping things in good working order doesn't usually include making things pretty or putting tools back where they belong or disposing of the junk parts.

On the farm, dust (and worse) is always the Super Hero who wins the day. Lucky for me, when I want things "just so," I can head to my part-time job at Hampton House Art & Framing. There, picture-perfect is the rule. Doing battle with that pesky speck of dust under the glass is not only acceptable, it's required. And, sooner or later, I *will* be the victor.

In the 60s, Malvina Reynolds wrote the song *Little Boxes*[13], purporting that houses and the people who live in them all tend look alike. Her descriptive *ticky-tacky* was actually put in the dictionary, being defined as *uninspired* or *monotonous sameness*. Is that what I want? Is boring monotony more alluring than the messy life I'm living here? The fact is, many of my best memories are of crazy stuff that just happened. Mistakes that made me laugh. Weird people. Unexpected joys and sorrows. I really don't want to smoosh those wild and wonderful oddities (messes) into cookie-cutter sameness, do I?

I left a cute little blue house in Charlotte, having no idea what farm life with Weldon would be like. Yes, much of it is gross to me, but it's real life—real, goofy, frustrating life, with nary a hint of ticky-tacky to be found.

Letting go of ways and habits (and little boxes) that are comfortable and normal to us isn't easy. But even old dogs can be taught new tricks. Years ago I learned three rules (tricks) for being a good missionary. The first: Be flexible; the second: Be flexible; and the third: Be flexible. These three rules have proved to be indispensable on the dairy farm. The ability to "go with the flow" is required when you're dealing with cows, crops, cats, and a farmer.

If I spend the last days of my life confined to an insipid room in a nursing home, I'll probably be whining about the sterile neatness of my surroundings. I'll secretly hope Weldon drags in a little yuck on the bottom of his shoes when he comes to visit. When he leaves, my eyes will lovingly caress the drawers he didn't quite close, and I'll chuckle at the door left slightly ajar.

Believing that there's a proper place for everything and that everything should be where it belongs wears me out. It probably drives Weldon a little crazy, too, but he never complains about who I am or what I do. I'm happy to report that I'm making progress in regressing to more slovenly ways. Progressing in regressing? Well, something like that. Little by little, I'm learning to celebrate the chaos that is life. I'm being flexible, opening my hands, and letting go. It feels good.

12

CRAP WON'T KILL YOU

*Always look to the good stuff in your life, otherwise you're
wasting what time you're given here, sulking about the crap
that in the end won't be anything to you.*

~Anonymous

I laughed when I recently came across the first Christmas
letter I wrote as a farmer's wife. Weldon and I had been
married for just three months, yet I used the word *crap* quite
freely. Here, in part, is what I wrote:

"Cindy's house sold in November and now all of her crap
has been added to Weldon's crap in his house. What a lot of crap.
The good news is that we have had new flooring installed
throughout the house, and we received lots of wonderful new
stuff (vs. crap) for our showers and wedding, so Weldon's house
is truly becoming our home."

Everyone has the proverbial crap to deal with. Even in
my pre-dairy-farm days, I had my share of frustrations and

inconveniences. Seeing and smelling the real thing on a daily basis, however, opened up a whole new world to me. In the paragraphs that immediately follow, crap is actual manure—the solid waste that farm animals leave behind, wherever they go.

The milk cows stay in a concrete-floored lounging barn with free-stalls filled with sawdust for their bedding. They also have access to two outside feeding lots and plenty of fresh water. Every day Weldon takes the skid loader into these areas and pushes the excrement into a manure pit. Before he has finished his job, the crap is flying again.

On any given day, each of our milk cows gives six to seven gallons of milk and produces about 100 pounds of crap (also known as high-value organic fertilizer). Landing on concrete, the manure makes quite a splat, and if any of the livestock has been lucky enough to escape the barn for a few luxurious minutes, she will be sure to leave her calling card in the barnyard or along the road.

While I'm milking cows, nothing is as disgusting as when a cow does her 'duty' and said 'duty' finds a landing spot on my body or my clothes.

"Eeeuwww. Is there crap in my hair?"

"No, I don't see any," Weldon calmly responds, as he carefully studies the top of my head.

"Look again. I felt it land right about here."

One morning after chores were finished and before we got to the house for breakfast, Weldon decided we should take a quick drive up Pilot Mountain to take advantage of the beautiful Carolina-blue sky and the hint of warmer weather wafting on the breeze. He didn't have to twist my arm. We hopped in the car and headed to the state park. As we pulled into the upper parking area, I looked down and saw crusty splashes of crap on my jeans. *And I'm going out in public like this? What a country hick!* No one noticed or cared.

Some people actually live in garbage dumps, complete with human and animal feces. For them, crap may cause sickness or death; for the rest of us, crap isn't deadly. Even on the dairy farm, we're blessed with the means to keep clean and healthy, so cow poo can be washed away without harmful repercussions.

If there's a cow pie in the area, I will step in it. This seems to be one of Murphy's laws for me. Although I've heard more than one person say they used to step in cow pies (on purpose) with their bare feet, this is not what I'm talking about. When my well-clad foot lands in the squishy stuff, I immediately scrape the yuck off in the grass or gravel. Then I use the water hose to wash off the residue. Rather than wallowing in the crap, I get rid of it. So why do I find myself wallowing in little aggravations, playing them over and over again in my head? Just as I wash the manure from my boots and clothes, I need to get rid of the poo that tries to make itself at home in my heart and mind.

Sometimes I think I've washed all the icky stuff from my boots, but then I get a whiff of that familiar stink. Upon closer inspection, I find a chunk of manure smooshed in the tread or on the back of the heel. The solution is simple: go back to the hose and rewash the boot.

Thinking I've dealt with negative feelings or situations, I'm surprised to see them pop up again. It doesn't make sense to boohoo over the realization; that would be wallowing. Instead, I deal with it again, and maybe again and again. But it can't hang around for too long. Instead of a water hose, I pray, sing, and maybe throw in a little shouting for good measure. I read a Bible verse or two and take time to formulate true and positive statements about the situation. I'm a big girl. I really don't have to let negative nonsense ruin a perfectly good day.

Smelly dung is easier to deal with than the crap of abusive people, family struggles, or serious life situations that seemingly have no answers. If the worst I have to deal with is cow droppings, I'm blessed, indeed.

While writing this chapter, I learned that *manure* is also a verb. It means to enrich by the application of manure. When the pile gets big (remember, 100 pounds of waste from each cow, every day), Weldon spreads the so-called waste over his fields, making the fields better. This stinky stuff is improving the farm. With my new knowledge of this verb, should a visitor ask where Weldon is, I'll respond, "He's out manuring." That just makes me chuckle.

If we know how to make good use of it, is it possible that crap can make our lives better? Yes! Handled correctly (eeuuww), and seen in the right light (usually long after the fact), problems add 'high value' to our lives.

Read the story of Joseph in the book of Genesis. He was dealt an incredible amount of junk. His brothers were jealous of him and sold him into slavery. Pharaoh's wife told lies about him, causing him to be thrown in jail. Cellmates who were released from prison forgot their promises to him. Through it all, Joseph kept his eyes on God, held onto a positive attitude, and lived with integrity. The end result? He was raised to second-in-command in Egypt and ultimately saved the lives of his father and brothers.

If it's not a case of being in danger of physical harm or death, then crap won't kill you. You are stronger than crap. Really, you are. But, if you should find yourself in the loblolly, remember that wallowing is optional! You don't have to settle in and call it home. Climb out of the slop, and you'll be stronger and better than before you slipped in.

I've learned that crap won't kill me, but I do wonder if the stench of the farm is clinging to me and has permeated the house. When you come to visit, I may pose the question, "Does it smell bad in here?" You'll tell me the truth, won't you?

13

MY GO-TO SMILE

Frame your mind to mirth and merriment, which bars a
thousand harms and lengthens life.

~William Shakespeare[14]

Awww, look at the sweet baby kitties." Sitting on the hay barn floor, I was enthralled by the antics of two new kittens. Weldon deftly ascertained that the black and white one was a female and the smaller black one was a male. I watched them play until names popped into my head. "I'm going to name this bold and inquisitive one Kit Carson. And maybe her timid little brother will grow into his name: Big Boy." Thus began my love affair with cats and kittens.

When I moved to the farm, I noticed that the cats were fed but otherwise mostly ignored and, consequently, quite wild. Not many of them had names, either, but I soon remedied that: Hatfield and McCoy (two males who couldn't walk by each other without snarling, spitting, and fighting), Tripod (a little female who lost a leg in a mowing accident), and Big Mama (a capable and willing mother to any kitten needing a little extra nourishment or snuggles). One by one, I named them all, and most of them became quite tame.

Now, each new kitten is carefully watched and coddled and given a suitable name. All (at one time as many as 50) are fed and snuggled, cared for and doctored, and none escapes our attention, whether they want it or not.

It doesn't matter how busy we are, chore time always includes kitty time, and everyone gets in on the fun. Weldon's mom isn't a big fan of cats, but she sits on the hay barn floor, cleaning the eyes of little Uno (the only kitten she has ever named). Weldon is off to the milk barn, carrying a big cat in his arms. Kitty VanHalen sits on Pat's shoulder as she gets ready to feed the calves, and I'm crawling over old tires and broken machinery in one of the junk piles, trying to find Spitz's new babies.

I hadn't had much previous experience with cats or kittens, but after two years on the farm, I wrote on my blog (farmmuse.blogspot.com) that watching them was a highlight of my life. My friend Carolyn commented, "The kittens are the highlight of your life on the farm? I'm gonna tell Weldon!" That made me smile but, truly, I was captivated by the little rascals.

The charming antics above are, perhaps, an odd introduction to this fact: life is hard.

First, life can be physically demanding. Duties inside and outside seem to be never-ending. I've seen Weldon sweating and grunting over more than one job he's tackled. He's farmed his entire life, but getting older means things that used to be easy are now more difficult and take a little longer to do. Ibuprofen is his new best friend. For me, having spent most of my life doing indoor work, outside chores give me a fair share of aches and pains and bruises, too. Bedtime is *my* new best friend—and I can't believe I'm admitting that to you.

Next, our thoughts can make life seem more difficult than it really is. I over-think just about everything and pay for it by getting down on myself and unhappy with life in general.

Quite early in our marriage, Weldon noticed this in me. One day he asked, "Are you okay?" I responded, "I'm just in a funk." Then I had to explain that a funk is a depressed state of mind. Yes, it can also mean an offensive smell, and I suppose my sour attitude emits some of that, too. On more than one occasion, when feeling that I don't measure up to his mom's and sisters' various skills, I've said to Weldon, "You should have married a *real* farm girl." There's no basis for such faulty imaginations, but they have a way of popping into my head and sucking the joy out of life.

Then, there's the emotional aspect of life which can be burdensome at times. Weldon is a passionate guy, easily shedding tears when he hears a favorite song, reads a sad story, remembers happy events, or just looks at me. He says his tear ducts are defective because they leak too easily. Even my phlegmatic tendencies have been on a roller coaster since becoming a farmer's wife. A whole new world is stirring me to feel and react: swear at the cows, revel in Mother Nature's beauty, cry over deaths, sing goofy songs to get through mundane chores, and smile at the frivolities of the kitties.

Ta-da! I'm back full circle to the cats and kittens. They are my go-to smile. When life starts to feel like it's more than I can handle, I know what to do: get outside and purr along with my favorite furry friends.

As I head down the driveway, cats are sure to meet me, winding around my feet and making it difficult to walk. I take a seat on a log and watch the kittens carousing, rolling, and scrapping. Orange tabbies, black and white tuxedos, spotted and speckled and adorable (too many to hold in my lap) vie for my attention. I run my fingers through their fur, pull their tails, rub their necks, and scratch their tummies. I hear the sound of Iris's motor in my ear as I gently pull her sharp little claws from my shoulder. I laugh out loud as Hansel and Gretel tumble off the log and continue their shenanigans on the ground. Yup, I'm smiling!

What about you? Where do you find that ray of sunshine when life starts to weigh you down? If an answer doesn't immediately pop into your head, take time to think about what invariably puts a smile on your face. It may be a favorite person or a familiar place. Maybe it's a specific action, like taking a walk, calling a friend, or putting together a puzzle. There are many options, but you'll get to that happy place quicker if you know what your "go-to smile" is.

Meow.

14

WHAT YOU SEE IS WHAT YOU GET

*The beginning of love is the will to let those we love be
perfectly themselves, the resolution not to twist them to fit our
own image. If in loving them we do not love what they are, but
only their potential likeness to ourselves, then we do not love
them: we only love the reflection of ourselves we find in them.*

~Thomas Merton[15]

hen Weldon asked me to marry him, I said yes. We
were old (that is to say, mature) enough to know that
it wasn't necessary to date for years and years to see if
this was the road we should take. We felt confident that God had
led us to each other and we should get on with our lives ...
together.

A diamond engagement ring wasn't in the picture
(impractical on the farm and an expense we didn't want to incur),
but an idea for wedding bands popped into my head and I
searched online until I found a place that turned my idea into

reality.

The background band is white gold. Over that is a cut-out yellow gold band that proclaims a message. My ring says WELDON IS A GIFT ♥. Weldon wanted his to say DRINK MORE MILK, but, big meanie that I am, I refused to grant his wish. Hence, the words on his ring are CINDY IS A GIFT ♥ CINDY IS A GIFT ♥. Since Weldon's finger is quite a bit bigger than mine, the phrase had to be repeated on his ring, and it gives me opportunity to tell people that I'm twice the gift that he is.

A few weeks before the wedding, we met with Pastor Larry Bumgarner who would perform the ceremony. After a few minutes, he asked Weldon to leave. I think I got a little nervous. Without knowing anything about me, Pastor Larry spoke words that went straight to my heart and have been an encouragement to me through the years. He also made a few observations about Weldon: "What you see is what you get. Weldon is a hardworking, honest man. He's not flashy and he won't try to impress anyone. He's just who he is."

What you see is what you get? Well, not exactly. From day one, I definitely saw the hardworking, kind, honest man. But while dating, I also saw a man who spent one day of almost every weekend with me. Every other Saturday or Sunday, Weldon milked the cows earlier than usual, made the two-hour drive to Charlotte, spent the day with me, and then made the two-hour drive back to the farm to milk the cows a little later than usual.

On the opposite weekends, I went to the farm. I didn't have cows to milk, so I could usually spend the whole weekend. His mom fixed a bed for me in her living room and, between morning and evening chores, Weldon showed me the farm and took me to explore many of the surrounding areas. I was impressed! This guy was really making an effort to spend time with me.

The Weldon I saw in those get-acquainted months drove an old rusty, dented pickup with a sagging headliner. However, it was clean, both inside and out, and he obviously kept it in good running order since it could make that one-hundred mile trip every other weekend.

He always wore a pair of khakis, a nice striped or plaid shirt, clean work boots, and a farmer-style baseball cap. During one of Weldon's first trips to Charlotte, I took him to meet my daughter Anna at her job. She later told me that, from a distance, she saw a man wearing a "different-looking" cap, and she knew it was Weldon and me. What? True! [Side note: A trucker cap or a "gimme" cap is so-called because it is given away as a free promotional item. Thank you, wikipedia[16].] Weldon's caps advertise bull semen, seed corn, or other farm-related products. And, yes, there's a slight physical difference between a baseball cap and the "gimme" caps that Weldon sports. He wasn't stylish, but he was always neat and clean.

When the wedding and weekend honeymoon were over, our weekly day together was over as well. The leisurely man I knew, making special time for me during those premarital months, disappeared. It's true that Sundays continue to be somewhat more relaxed than the rest of the week, but they rarely have that special one-on-one feeling that marked our getting-to-know-you time.

And that clean pickup? After we were married, his sister Pat confided, "I knew something was going on when I saw Weldon washing the truck and cleaning out the interior." The truck hasn't been clean since our dating days. A few years into our marriage, Weldon asked me to drive the pickup down to the lower fields for him. I was happy to oblige but, in the process, a favorite pair of capris got a grease stain that refused to come out. Lesson learned: Don't get into the truck (or any other farm vehicle, for that matter) until you've changed into work clothes.

On Sundays or for special events, Weldon's dress code is the same as during our dating days. For everything else, it's old, tattered jeans and shirts and work boots that definitely have that lived-in look. I understand, but that doesn't mean I like it. In the middle of fixing a piece of broken equipment, he may have to make a trip to town for parts. "You're going like that? Maybe you should change your clothes." No, he doesn't have time for such silliness. Does anyone at the hardware store notice or care? No. Along the same line, when Weldon stretches out his arms for a hug, I'm leery of snuggling in too close for fear of what will get transferred to my hair or clothes.

"Weldon, do you remember when we were dating? We spent an entire day together every week. We ate out. We went places. We *did* things. What happened?"

"Well," he replied. "We were courting. We're not courting anymore."

I was shocked. "Have you not read 'the books'? 'The books' say you must continue courting throughout your marriage to keep the romance alive."

He humphed.

Every now and then I remind him he should start courting again, but I realize the business of farming doesn't leave much time for day trips or inconsequential matters like a clean vehicle. The truck runs just as well when the seat is loaded with tools, rags, shotgun shells, corn cobs, truck parts, an extra hoodie, and any number of receipts and catalogs. "Just move that stuff over and slide in here, sweetie."

Through our years together, I've come to know the *real* Weldon, and I'm happy with the man he is. My wedding band says it all: "Weldon is a gift." He may not always meet my little hopes and expectations, but he is always the real deal-a gift.

"What you see is what you get." Hmmm. I'm guessing Pastor Larry was speaking of Weldon's heart, not his clothes or his ability to impress. "He's just who he is." If only I lived with such integrity.

15

HEY! I'M WORKING HERE

Dear children, let's not merely say that we love each other;
let us show the truth by our actions.

~1 John 3:18

During my years in Charlotte, I was the receptionist/administrative assistant in a young, technology-based firm. The owner and his eager, go-get-'em employees would often stay working into the evening hours. I, on the other hand, headed for the door when five o'clock rolled around. One particular afternoon, I entered the elevator, anxious to get down to the parking lot and point my car toward home. The doors were closing when the boss jumped in and exclaimed, "Don't you love this job? I bet you hate to leave at the end of the day." I rejected his supposition by saying, "No, actually, I love going home." He didn't fire me.

The farm has its own schedule (although I use the term very loosely). The radio announcer awakens us while it's still dark outside. We roll out of bed and pull on the same dirty work clothes we took off the night before. After a hug and a kiss, we go our separate ways to start our personal morning routines.

Weldon sits at the kitchen table having a cold, refreshing glass of orange juice and a piece of toast slathered in ooey-gooey homemade jam. He scoops it out by the teaspoonful, making sure each bite has sufficient sweetness. He gives yesterday's newspaper a final survey and checks his computer for the day's weather forecast.

I brew a cup of coffee and head to the living room, snuggling the warm mug close to my heart. This is God-and-me time. It includes reading a portion from the Bible, pondering the day's message from a devotional, and maybe jotting a few notes in my journal. I've started my days like this for many years, and it always helps prepare me, mentally and emotionally, for whatever the day may hold.

His morning routine finished, Weldon heads out to give the heifers their silage, water the livestock, and get the cows into the holding pen in preparation for milking. I follow a few minutes later to feed the cats. They all need backs petted, ears scratched, and tails pulled. If calves need to be bottle-fed, that chore is next on the to-do list. It won't be long before we get to the actual milking of cows.

This scenario is repeated again in about twelve hours, but then it's called evening chores. After a delicious and nutritious supper, I wash the dishes, put up my feet and relax, or do whatever I feel like doing. No, I'm sorry. That was in my previous life. In this life, after a delicious and nutritious supper, I wash the dishes, put on my work clothes, and head out to chores.

The evening tasks differ slightly from the morning's, but they still revolve around cows, calves, and cats and also include getting everything settled down for the night. I remain focused on each individual duty and like to see them done precisely, neatly, and in order.

Friends, neighbors, and other farmers know that if they need to see Weldon, they can find him, morning or evening, down around the barn. That's good for them, but an aggravation for me, because I don't have "Visitors" penciled in on my chore-time schedule.

What's this I see? A pickup. A man and a few kids get out. Weldon stops to talk to the Salvadorean guy whom I have seen on numerous occasions, always at chore time.

"Hola! You have corn?"

Weldon returns the greeting, speaking loudly, slowly, and using broken English. "Yes, corn in fields." He waves his arm widely toward the field across the road. "You bring sacks? Bags?"

Of course not. So Weldon walks to the abandoned well-house and retrieves a few old sacks. (Nothing is ever thrown away on the farm. You never know when you might need that old, broken, useless piece of whatever.) "Here. Get corn. I milk cows now."

I'm thinking, "Good! That didn't take too long. Could we please go to the milk parlor now and milk the cows? We have a schedule to keep, you know." I can't seem to shake the habit of wanting to get my job done so I can go home. But Weldon has the right attitude. He knows that people are important, whereas I tend to see them as interruptions to my well-planned agenda.

When I first came to the farm, Weldon told me that he hadn't had a vacation in seven years. I didn't know how to handle that information, especially after seeing how many hours he works every day. Every day. Sundays included. How could he go seven years without a vacation?

The light finally dawned on me: People are his escape, his diversion, even if for only a few minutes. He listens to them. He helps them. He teaches them. He *enjoys* them!

Me? I'm standing in the background, anxiously tapping my foot. *Hey! Can't you see we're working here? We need to get these cows milked so I can get back to the house.* Not letting a clock rule my life is one of the most difficult adjustments I've had to make on the dairy farm (along with all the other most difficult adjustments I'll whine about in the stories that follow).

Ever so slowly, I'm realizing it doesn't do any good to get all huffy about an interruption, be it human, animal, or mechanical. We'll get the chores done, and we'll get back to the house ... sooner or later.

I may not be a people person, but people are important. We'll never regret the kind words we speak or the time we spend in helping others. It's not a hardship to look people in the eye, greet them with sincerity, and actually "be there" for them. Weldon is a natural at this. Everyone knows he has a listening ear, an understanding heart, and the ability to give them the knowledge or advice they're seeking. Or the corn.

Instead of inwardly groaning when people come to see Weldon at chore time, I can smile, be attentive, or go back to playing with the kitties. The chores will get done and, in the meantime, someone is being helped or encouraged.

The next time Mr. Santiago comes, maybe I'll go find some empty bags for him.

"Gracias."

"De nada."

16

IN OVER MY HEAD

The battles that count aren't the ones for gold medals. The
struggles within yourself—the invisible, inevitable battles
inside all of us—that's where it's at.

~Jesse Owens[17]

S tarting a new phase of life (whether a change in location or career, starting a family, or heading off on a great adventure) is quite a bit like marriage. Both begin with a flush of …. Wait, that sounds too much like a potty/farm word. Both begin with a blush of anticipation for the fresh chapter that is about to be written. Things tend to be exciting and scary at the same time. For me, it was a double whammy: I got married and I moved from the city to a dairy farm.

My first full year on the farm was spent getting to know Weldon in his natural habitat and familiarizing myself with the farm. It was a good year! There was a peacefulness about it (except when the cows got out) and a joy in watching the seasons unfold in a country setting.

The honeymoon is over, and there's not much time for sitting on the porch swing with a sweet kitten on my lap. Now I'm a quasi farmhand, milking cows and helping with other outside chores. The farm is my new home and, yes, often times it scares me and even makes me wonder if I can keep doing this crazy stuff. Let me tell you the frightful story of one little calf.

A calf had just been born, but the amniotic sac clung to her head, and her nose lay in the pool of fluid. Weldon happened by, noticed the dangerous situation, jumped into the pen, and tore the sac away. He saved her from certain death, and Pat christened her Lucky Lucy.

Six months later, the phone rang at 11:45 p.m., waking me from an unusually deep sleep. It was Pat. I hung up the phone, stumbled across the room to find my clothes, all the while mumbling the info to Weldon. "Pat heard calves. Hmm, maybe older calves? She thinks one has fallen in the unh…." (In my not-quite-awake stupor, I couldn't remember the name of the icky place.)

RING! It was Pat again, verifying, "Yes, a calf is in the manure pit. The manure pit! Hurry!" In a flash, all the lights are on, we're in our clothes, and we're out the door.

Weldon jumps into the skid loader, stopping to get his big, heavy towing chain. Pat, with flashlight in hand, opens the gate and I, shivering in the cold and fear of the unknown, shine my flashlight over the area. Weldon drives to the manure pit, and Pat and I follow with our lights pushing back the dark. Sure enough, a calf was flailing in the concrete pit that holds the sloppy water and manure that's pushed off the feed lot each day.

Careful not to fall in himself, Weldon struggles with the calf and the heavy chain, finally securing the chain around the calf's neck. At the same time, Pat wrestles the other end of that heavy chain around the bucket of the skid loader. I hold two flashlights, sob quietly, and pray. When the chain is attached to calf and bucket, Weldon hops back into the skid loader, slowly backs up, and pulls the calf out of the slimy goo. *Thank you, Jesus!* SPLAT! A gross gob of goo lands on the hood of my sweatshirt.

Eeeuuuw. Please don't fall into my eyes.

Weldon unwraps the chain from calf and bucket. He scoops the calf into the bucket, and delivers her back to the calf shed. We wash the yuck off her and cover her with plenty of fresh hay to help her get warm. A mere hour after that first call, our work is done and we trudge back to our homes.

It was a crazy, scary night, but I didn't pack my bags to head back to more comfortable and familiar surroundings. I just washed up and climbed into bed with my farmer.

The next morning we ascertained that the rescued calf was none other than Lucky Lucy. Weldon promptly changed her name to Hapless Hannah.

I couldn't have imagined that moving a hundred miles would so drastically change my life. In many ways it feels like I'm living on a different planet. My favorite work sweatshirt says it all: *I'm in over my head.* Truly, life on a dairy farm is deep, and at times I feel like I'm going down. It has stretched me to the breaking point, but it hasn't broken me. Yes, I've broken down in tears. Yes, I've asked myself if I made a horrible mistake. Yes, I'm in over my head, but the grace of God holds me up.

Life isn't a still-life painting, an inanimate creation. On the contrary, it's continuous action and change. According to Romans 5:3, our struggles are good for us, because they help us grow. Children master the art of riding a bicycle by falling, getting up and back on the bike, falling, and doing it all over again. College students become graduates in their chosen field by making it through one year at a time, choosing serious study and determination over partying the nights away. Newlyweds don't stay newlyweds but are transformed by years of chiseling and refining to become the couple celebrating their 50th wedding anniversary. Ask any of them if it was easy. "No, it took a lot of work." But was it worth it? "Look at me now! I wouldn't change a thing."

Because of the unsettling fluctuations of life, we learn to live by faith. You might say, "Wait a minute. I don't live by faith. I live by my skill, by the seat of my pants, by my own hard work. Faith has nothing to do with it." Actually, we all have things, people, or ideas we trust in and pin our hopes on. If we don't believe that we can do something, we don't do anything. Children just know they can ride a bike; the student is convinced he can become a doctor; the married couple does battle together and says, "We will get through this. Come hell or high water, we *will* get through this." We're born with a go-for-it attitude (faith, if you will), but the rigors of life do their best to beat it out of us.

Since life is much bigger than we are, it's not surprising to feel like we're in over our heads. Fortunately, we're not alone and we're not unique in our feelings or experiences. Asking for help or advice or simply sharing our fears and frustrations with a friend can be the life jacket that keeps our heads above water until our feet get back on solid ground.

When I run out of steam, when I find myself in deep doo-doo, when I've lost faith in my own abilities, I need God's strength and wisdom to keep me afloat. Look at these buoys from Psalm 37. Verse 5: "Commit everything you do to the Lord. Trust him, and he will help you." Verses 23 and 24: "The Lord directs the steps of the godly. He delights in every detail of their lives. Though they stumble, they will never fall, for the Lord holds them by the hand." Verse 39: "The Lord rescues the godly; he is their fortress in times of trouble." Knowing what God says emboldens me more than the best self-help book on my shelf.

No one said life would be easy. When you're running out of options, God's promises are a great source of encouragement. He's cheering us on. There's no going back, so dive in and keep stretching toward the prize.

17

JUDGE NOT

To love someone is to strive to accept that person exactly the way he or she is, right here and now.

~Fred Rogers[18]

The footwear of choice on the farm is heavy, steel-toed work boots. There was no niche in my brain for this fact when I first met Weldon, but it was definitely his boots that caught my eye (and not in a positive way). Yes, they were clean, but work boots? On a first date?

As it turns out, Weldon wears his work boots until they fall apart. He also has a newer pair of boots to wear to church and, apparently, on first dates. The day we married, I was pleased to see him waiting for me at the altar with black dress shoes on his feet. I later learned that he keeps them hidden away in a box in his closet and dons them for weddings and funerals. That was the extent of his shoe wardrobe. No slippers, no flip flops, no penny loafers.

It seems like he would opt for comfort once in a while, but no. First thing in the morning, Weldon puts on his work clothes and his boots. When he comes in at night, does he get those heavy things off his feet and wiggle his toes? No, he wears them until he's ready to hop into the shower before bedtime. I understand now, of course, that there's a method to his madness. Boots are difficult to get off and on, and if he needs to get outside in a hurry, he's always ready.

Flashback to a church gathering on a cold Minnesota winter evening in the early '70s. A man gets out of his seat and walks to the front. Will he preach or sing or make an announcement? I don't know and I don't care, because I'm completely focused on his footwear—great big bunny boots. Yes, it was cold outside, and yes, the snow was deep, and yes, bunny boots were popular and appropriate for our area. *Are you kidding? You should take those big clodhoppers off when you come into church!* That's what was going on in my head, and that's all I remember of that evening.

Fast-forward twenty-some years. I'm an office assistant in a snazzy start-up company in Charlotte and I'm the one wearing bunny boots. No, not literally, but that's how it feels. My clothes aren't fashionable, my car is nothing special, and I don't receive invitations to the in-crowd parties. Since I was good at judging others, it was easy to suppose that others were judging me, too.

Now here I am on a farm, where stuff is old and getting older with every rising and setting of the sun. New, clean, and fashionable rarely exist on a 200-year-old farm, especially since Weldon is a master at fixing, tinkering, and keeping things running. We had been married just a couple of years when he had to purchase a new manure spreader, and he turned the event into a celebration. He hoisted the garden table (complete with umbrella) and chairs into the shiny red machine, and poured us each a glass of milk. My younger daughter Katie was here for a visit, so she took a picture as we toasted the big day.

I like new, clean, shiny. When we'd hop into the pickup to run an errand, I'd secretly hang my head in shame. Why? Because it's dented and rusty on the outside and a veritable junk pile on the inside. *We deserve better than this yucky old thing.* Try as I might, it was impossible to squish farm life into new, clean, shiny. Believe me, I tried.

It wasn't long before this judgmental attitude slithered beyond inanimate objects and wrapped itself around Weldon. You've already seen how I wanted him to follow all my household rules. Imagine my consternation when, although I'm living in a world I know nothing about, I caught myself brazenly thinking, *Things would run better if Weldon quit doing it like that (his way) and started doing it like this (my way).*

Because I put my tools away when I'm done using them, does that make me better than Weldon? If I mop the floors each week and sweep down the cobwebs at least once a month, does that make me more acceptable in your eyes? In my own eyes? That's some really messed up thinking, commonly known as *pride*. C.S. Lewis[19] wrote, "Pride is spiritual cancer: it eats up the very possibility of love, or contentment, or even common sense."

Contempt piles up like garbage and begins to stink. It's time to take the garbage out, and, as I already mentioned, that's my job. Fortunately, the gentle prodding of beloved Bible verses helps me with the daunting task. John 7:24 says we shouldn't judge according to outward appearances. Luke 6:37 puts it like this: "Do not judge others, and you will not be judged. Do not condemn others, or it will all come back against you." After years of reading and "knowing" these verses, I'm taking them to heart and asking God to make them real in my life.

Humility is the antidote for pride, but it doesn't come easily. To be humble is to be lowly and down-to-earth. We're all made of the same stuff—dust, according to the Bible. You can't get more down-to-earth than that. Romans 3:27 poses a thought-provoking question: What can we boast or brag about? Without being given time to mull it over in our heads, the question is answered for us: There's no room left for bragging. The "I'm better than you" attitude has been eliminated. In God's eyes, we're all the same. He has chosen each of us to be part of his family, not because of anything we've done, but because of his eternal love.

We're supposed to love and accept people as they are. God made them, they're living their life as they have chosen or doing the best they can with what they have. Heck! Maybe they're not even *trying* to do good. But God loves them just as they are. And he wants us to love them, too, and treat them with respect. "Most important of all, continue to show deep love for each other, for love covers a multitude of sins" (1 Peter 4:8). That's a tall order, impossible to fill on our own, but we have access to God's strength and marvelous wisdom.

I'm learning. I'm growing. Boots make good sense on a farm, and having good sense is better than looking good. My work garb is drab and often spattered with you-know-what, but if I go out to chores dressed as though I were going to my office job in Charlotte, even the cats and cows would snicker. The old machinery around here doesn't look snazzy, but frugal ways keep the dairy farm debt-free, and we can be proud of that.

I'm becoming more content with who I am and what I have. Riding through town in our even-older-now pickup, I'm every bit as carefree as the Clampetts[20] were when they rattled into Beverly Hills in their jalopy.

When I'm down-to-earth (and the farm keeps me close to the earth every day), I recognize the value of people and can care for them (love them!) as though they are next-of-kin. Humility has become a place of security where I don't need to prove or explain myself to you, and you don't need to prove yourself to me. Should we ever meet, I'm not going to look down on you or expect you to be someone you're not. I'll accept you as you are.

Wear your boots proudly. That's my new motto.

18

TODAY IS A GIFT

Ever since our forebears figured out that a dead seed will spring from the Earth, a mix between careful tending and damn luck, they've acknowledged that to live, and to breathe, and to eat is a gift. All of it, gift.

~Timothy Brown[21]

Cats and calves fed; cows milked and milk parlor washed down; half-gallon jug filled with fresh, cold milk for Weldon's breakfast; and now I'm merrily strolling back to the house. Opening the door, I sigh in relief. *Ahh, now I can get my day started.*

MY day. It slapped me upside the head. *Now I can get MY day started.* The book of Psalms says, "This is the day the Lord has made. We will rejoice and be glad in it." Ooops. This is the *Lord's* day. He made it, it's his, and if he gives me a small part in it (even lets me share it with cows), that's pretty awesome...and it changes my focus.

Since God is sharing this day with me, that makes it a gift, and everyone loves gifts. Birthday surprises, Christmas presents, a plate of cookies brought to the office, an invitation to see an exhibit at the museum—the list could go on and on.

Is it possible to receive a gift without a smile or a feeling of gladness? Perhaps what's given isn't exactly what we wanted or is the wrong size or we aren't allowed to eat it because of dietary restrictions. Yet, even in these less-than-ideal scenarios, the present is still received with a thankful smile because we see the heart of the giver.

Weldon's dear family (now *my* dear family) is constantly sharing their bounty with me, and that often translates into work. On Tuesday evening, Weldon's younger sister Beth stopped by with a box of apples. "I got these in Cana, Virginia. They make really good applesauce." The next morning, Edith drives up, opens her trunk, and brings two gallons of strawberries to the door. "How about some strawberries with your breakfast?" A few hours later, Pat calls, "Broccoli is on sale and I bought way too much. I'll share."

The goodies are all received with a smile on my face and gracious thanks, because I know their generosity is an outpouring of love. Unfortunately, my thoughts don't always follow the same pleasant path. "Well, there go my plans. Looks like I'll be stuck in the kitchen all day again."

Focus, Cindy. Focus! I can receive my family's generosity with self-centered groans or with open heart and hands. A few hours of happy work transform fruits and veggies into gifts that keep on giving. Strawberries are not only a delicious treat on our cereal for the next few mornings, but I make a batch of jam that will be a yummy treat when fresh strawberries aren't readily available. I set aside enough broccoli for supper, and I freeze the rest for another meal or two. Up to my elbows in all this domesticity, I peel and core the apples, set them on the stove to simmer, and breathe in the heavenly aroma of sugar and spice and everything nice. "Stuck in the kitchen" turns into a day of rejoicing.

The Bible says we should give thanks *for* everything and *in* everything. In so doing, we admit that God is God and we are not. He made the day, he knows the plans he has for us, we're in his hands. In the Old Testament, Job and his wife lost their oxen, donkeys, sheep, camels, most of their servants, and all of their children. His wife wanted to curse God, but Job asked her, "Should we accept only good things from the hand of God and never anything bad?" (This almost made me want to "suck it up" and quit writing this whiny book. Almost.) The message of Job is that God never leaves us. He is with us in sickness and health, in good times and bad, in life and death, and, yes, even in the milk parlor or the way-too-busy kitchen.

Recognizing each day as a gift is not a new idea. But seeing how I drag through some days, it's obvious that I'm not always acting according to what I believe. Rejoicing in farm life takes practice. Yes, I do exclaim "O, Lord!" quite often, but the words are usually uttered in exasperation more than from a grateful heart.

Along a similar vein, I've asked myself if I'm supposed to be thankful for a headache. Throughout my life, I've suffered from migraine headaches. During those years, I wondered if I should think of a migraine as some strange gift. Thankfully, my headaches are finally of the common variety, in that they don't make me sick and they usually respond quite nicely to aspirin. I'm truly glad that my headache isn't a migraine, but is it possible to simply be thankful for a headache without making the comparison? And why would I do that? Perhaps because I'm still alive and may live to see another day?

Barbara Johnson[22] wrote many humorous, inspirational books on the topic of finding joy in the crud. A quote I remember is, "Life is hard and then we die." Maybe it's time to reread some of her wisdom.

We've all heard stories of people looking back over a horrific event in life and seeing the blessing that resulted from it. This is "God stuff" that doesn't make sense to the human mind. Seeing everything as a gift (including the things that make me sad or mad or discouraged) isn't easy. Feeling like no one understands what I'm experiencing, or no one else has to deal with this kind of crap, is just a bunch of self-centered malarkey. My struggles are *not* unique. Everyone goes through trials and aggravations. When I remember that I'm not alone, that my woes are common to my neighbor and to you, it gives me courage and renewed hope and, yes, my heart feels lighter and more thankful.

Life is full of surprises and secrets longing to be discovered. Too often we're looking in the wrong places, hoping for flamboyant miracles instead of gladly receiving what's right in front of us. Use your imagination to unwrap that "gift" that feels cumbersome or even painful. Maybe it looks like dirty work boots or a reject from the thrift store. Take time to study this "gift." Once you get past the distractions, you may find you're holding something that will change your life.

Remembering that each day (today!) is freely given to me doesn't automatically turn my day around, but it does get me back to a place of truth. Remember what my wedding band says? *Weldon is a gift.* Over the years I've wondered, "If Weldon is a gift, does that make the farm a gift, too?" No! Say it isn't so! But, oh, the things I've experienced and learned, seen and savored, laughed and cried over. Yes, I'm beginning to see that the farm is somewhat like a great big present, specially chosen just for me. Really horrible wrapping paper, by the way.

19

WHOA IS ME

Talk happiness. The world is sad enough without your woe.
No path is wholly rough.

~Ella Wheeler Wilcox[23]

No, that's not a misspelling in this chapter's title. "Woe is me" is the saying we all know and love, but my mother has a friend who writes "*Whoa* is me." It makes me laugh and, at the same time, bemoan the state of the English language. Mulling over that little kink in the phrase, I realize the word *whoa* reveals a wisdom of its own.

Here are the simple definitions of the two words. *Woe* expresses sorrow, regret, or distress; w*hoa* commands slow down, stop, or don't go there.

When I'm feeling tired or a little headache-y, *Oh, woe is me* starts its nagging little chant. *Poor little me, I work so hard. No one really knows what I have to deal with.* I'm not the only one who knows how to throw a fabulous pity party, am I?

The trouble with pity parties is that no one shows up. I don't feel like working. I don't feel like creating. Leave me alone. Don't ask me to do anything today. Can't you see I'm tired and cranky? And thus it begins, that slippery slope heading down to Woe-Is-Me Land. It can just as accurately be called Whoa-Is-Me Land because life comes to a grinding halt. I can hear the brakes screeching. Time is wasted, never to be regained.

This morning the radio rudely awakened us at 5:30. Weldon rolled over, shut it off, and promptly went back to sleep. I rolled over, rolled back the other way, and began to fuss in my head. *If he's not gonna get up when the radio tells us it's time to rise and shine, why does he set it? He falls back to sleep, but I can't.* Despite knowing that Weldon's morning inaction was nothing new (his dad used to come and pound on the side of the house to get him out of bed), I continued my mental fuming. Finally, I get up—on the wrong side of the bed, of course. Instead of being glad to have some extra reading time, resentment is rumbling in the back of my head.

I drag through morning chores and plod home to make breakfast. Weldon comes in a little later, we eat, and he's ready to head back outside to tackle some more of the day's chores. He stops at the sink, gives me a kiss, and says, "Thanks for breakfast, sweetie. I love you."

"I love you, too." I echo his words, but my heart isn't in it. *Of course you love me. I cook for you and wash the dishes, do everything around the house, and help you with your work. What's not to love?*

Here's the fact: Weldon doesn't get up at the sound of the morning alarm. End of story. By making it all about poor me, lies start rushing into my head until the morning's non-event is inflated like a novelty balloon worthy of Macy's Thanksgiving Day Parade. *You made the biggest mistake of your life when you married a dairy farmer. You have no friends. You blew it when you walked away from Haiti. You're pathetic.* And not one of these thoughts has anything to do with the alarm clock! Oh, woe is me!

God says I should take every thought captive (2 Corinthians 10:5). He says I'm master over what goes on in my head. I rule my thoughts; they shouldn't rule me. I have to replace the lies with words that are true and hopeful.

According to Hebrews 6:19, hope is an unbreakable spiritual lifeline, a strong and trustworthy anchor. Here are a few synonyms of hope: expectancy, trust, anticipation … and its opposites: despair, suspicion, doubt, and cynicism. Yup, those last words describe my morning quite well. I have to remind myself that my hope is in the Lord!

Can we actually walk in truth and hope? That is, of course, exactly what being a Christian is all about. Whatever is going on around us, whatever is going on inside our heads, God's word is the way, the truth, and the life worth living. Calling to mind God's love and truth changes my dull, uncaring ruminations to joy and peace. Ruminating … that really should be left to the cows.

I've experienced feeling down in the dumps and then getting an unexpected call to spend time with a friend. It's amazing how quickly the self-centered blues vanish. "Oh, that sounds like fun. I can be ready in half an hour. See you then." Is it possible to carry this same enthusiasm into a discouraging day by simply remembering God's invitation to walk with him? Yes! His is the best invitation, the best plan for every day of my life.

I developed a little arsenal to help me defeat the oh-woe-is-me syndrome. If you struggle with self-pity, these weapons might help you, as well.

The first and most important weapon is *truth*. God's word is truth. Write down a few verses of hope and encouragement. (Do this on a sunshiny, happy day because you won't feel like doing it when the blues hit). Keep them handy so you can pull them out as soon as you receive an invitation to a pity party. Don't believe everything that tiptoes across your mind. Check it out. Tell it to stop. "Whoa there, you ugly little rumor. That isn't true. You will not rule my day." I can hear Barney Fife[24] saying, "Nip it. Nip it in the bud."

Next comes vocal *thankfulness*. Yes, out loud works best. "Yippee! I'm recognizing what goes on in my head." Say it a few times, with conviction, and then find at least one other true thing to put in your heart and mind to contemplate during the day. It can be anything, big or small, that puts a smile of gratitude on your face: good health, someone dear to you, pizza, a favorite memory. Words of gratitude have a marvelous way of snowballing, and vocalizing your thanks makes a huge difference. There's no room for "poor little me" in a thankful heart.

Now it's time to take *action*. Get out of your head and, if at all possible, get your body moving. Turn on music that demands a little shimmying and shaking. Take an invigorating walk. Tackle a job or hobby that you've been putting off for ages. I'm not saying you have to break into a sweat but, if it helps, go for it. You know what works for you. If you're at work and don't have the luxury of taking a physical break, you can find creative ways to throw heart and soul into what's in front of you. Positive action speaks louder than the sob stories in your head.

And, finally, my *secret weapon*: cookies! Eating (especially cookies) makes me feel better, at least for a few minutes. Unfortunately, when my tongue has discovered and dislodged the last bits hiding between my teeth, I want another cookie. Oh, woe is me. Okay, cookies may not be the best remedy for self-pity. However, after employing truth, thankfulness, and a brisk walk through the woods or around the neighborhood, rewarding yourself with a cookie is totally acceptable. Trust me on this one.

20

THINGS DIE HERE

Reality is merely an illusion, albeit a very persistent one.

~Albert Einstein[25]

A first-time mama cat might leave her babies too soon or have too many babies to give each one all the milk and attention it needs. Such was the case with baby Tootsie. She developed a slight case of diarrhea, mama wasn't keeping her clean, and, being the runt, she wasn't getting enough of that life-giving fluid. But Tootsie was doing her best to survive in this cruel world. The wind whipped mercilessly through the barnyard and the cold air birthed goosebumps on my exposed flesh, so I scooped up little Tootsie and whisked her to the house where I could wrap her in a towel and make her all warm and cozy.

Our typical method of caring for a sickly kitten is to put a towel in a box and set the box on its side in the bathtub. The kitty has a secure place to rest but can venture out into the tub to eat and take care of business. On her third morning of house arrest,

Tootsie ate a little and even tried to follow me around the kitchen until it was time to put her back in the bathtub.

When I came in that afternoon, I bustled around with supper preparations and then realized I hadn't heard any sounds from the bathroom. I hurried in to check on Tootsie, but she didn't move or make any noise. I could tell she hadn't eaten anything, and there was no pee or poop in the tub. "You poor dear." I stroked her fur one final time, but she surprised my already-aching heart with the slightest turn of her head. She was cold, so I bundled her up in the towel, snuggled her close, and rocked her until she breathed her last and Weldon came in for supper.

Tootsie isn't the first kitty to die on the farm. In spite of our best efforts, some are sickly from the start. Others go off exploring and never return. There were two years when the local coyote population decimated our feline family. Cars, trucks, and farm machinery have been the end of a cat or two or three. No matter when or how a cat or kitten dies, it's heartbreaking to all of us, but maybe especially to me.

One Sunday morning, Weldon informed us that a bull calf had been born. He got the skid loader, picked up the calf in the bucket, and brought it to the pen. After feeding the cats, I went back to the house to get breakfast ready and to prepare for church.

After church, Weldon went to feed the new baby calf. He had been out for about thirty minutes when I heard him open the door. "Cindy?" he called. "Come here, please."

He stood outside on the porch, holding the door open while I stood inside, and he told me his story. "I went out to feed the calf. He took the bottle greedily, chugging down the milk. He finished half the bottle, made a few raucous bleats ... b-aa-aa-aa, b-aa-aa-aa ... fell over, gasped, and died."

"What? Are you kidding?" I couldn't believe it. He told me the same story again, this time ending, "In 60 years on the farm, I've never seen such a thing. I'm going to bury him now."

Weldon thought that perhaps the calf's esophagus was deformed, thus sending the milk to his lungs instead of his stomach. Later, when Weldon told the bizarre story to the veterinarian, she surmised, because of the suddenness of it, that maybe the calf died from a heart attack.

One by one, all of our dogs (Weldon's Rocky, Missy,and Molly, and my Jasmine) died quite peacefully of old age or complications thereof.

A grown cow might die or have to be put down because of a malady.

With his family gathered round, even Weldon's dad died here.

I remember the time my younger daughter Katie was visiting us. One evening after chores, Weldon, she, and I were in the office, each of us busy at our computers. A frightful scrambling, crashing sound in the woods behind the house, followed by a crying yowl, startled us. Katie jerked her head up, asking the fearful question, "What the heck was that?"

"Oh, no! A coyote must have caught a fawn," I exclaimed as I jumped up and anxiously threw open the window.

Katie's face paled. "What?"

"No." Weldon calmly negated my rash statement. "It was probably a fawn calling to its mom who had dashed through the woods, forgetting that her youngster would have difficulty keeping up." Neither of us really bought his story, but it helped dispel the dark phantasm that had sneaked in through the open window.

The next morning, Katie and I were relaxing, talking about anything and everything. Out of the blue, she said, "That's why I don't like the farm so much. Things die here, and that makes me sad."

She's absolutely right. Death is a big part of why I find the farm a difficult place in which to get comfortable. Many times I long for my sterile life in Charlotte. "Things" and people died in Charlotte, too, but they were things and people to whom I felt no attachment. I could ignore death or, when disaster struck a person or country, I could send up a prayer and merrily go on with my life.

Death happens all around us, wherever we are. Death is

part of life, but not generally the part I like to think about or deal with. King Solomon, in the book of Ecclesiastes, said there's a time for everything, including death. We see it reflected in nature: Fall sends the advance warning, "Get ready, stuff is going to die;" then winter sets in and, from many outward appearances, it seems that stuff has, indeed, died.

Winter is followed by the good news of spring: "Arise, my love." It looked like death, but now there's new life peeking out everywhere. You can't stop death and death can't stop life.

Death makes us sad. It marks the end of a baby kitten or a lumbering elephant, a beautiful flower or a majestic redwood. Most devastatingly, it marks the end of a human life. In each case, we might lament, "What a waste."

This is the area where I pity those who don't believe in the work that God has done for us. The human mind simply says, "Stuff dies; end of story." But the same miracle of life-out-of-death that is revealed in nature is also seen in the spiritual world. Here's the good news (1 Corinthians 15:54,55): "Then, when our dying bodies have been transformed into bodies that will never die, this Scripture will be fulfilled: 'Death is swallowed up in victory. O death, where is your victory? Oh, death, where is your sting?'" It looks like the end, but we have the hope of a new beginning, a life that will never end.

"This farm is killing me." If I haven't said it out loud, I've definitely mumbled it in my head. What about you? What's killing you? What's aggravating you to the breaking point? What's making you sob on the inside or shed big alligator tears on the outside? Whatever it is, remember: Hope triumphs.

Things die here, but there's the promise of new, forever life that will never die. That's good news...even on the farm.

21

HO HUM

Every wakeful step, every mindful act is the direct path to awakening. Wherever you go, there you are.

~Buddha[26]

See Bessie. See Bessie eat. She nuzzles the deliciously-fermented silage in the feeding trough.

See Belle. See Belle run. "Come on, Bessie. The other girls are already scampering in front of the big hay barn. Let's get out of here and join the party."

Are cows fickle? Fickle is a cute little word, but its synonyms are quite ugly: capricious, inconsistent, unstable. Maybe they're just bored, although being bored doesn't paint a pretty picture either: weary and restless because of a lack of interest. Ho hum.

Believe it or not, I'm learning from these aggravating cows. I can embrace the sameness of ordinary days like Bessie does, or I can label my life boring and join Belle in raising a little dust. Boring? On the farm? Yes, I admit it. Sometimes I'm longing for something I can't quite put my finger on. Nothing catches my imagination. I keep moving, doing what needs doing, but my heart isn't in it. Ho hum.

Many city dwellers would happily change places with me because, you know, the grass is greener over here. "I would love to live with the beauty and serenity of nature right outside my front door. You surely are lucky!" I hear their comments and, after guffawing on the inside, I realize their words are true. I really am blessed.

You've already learned that I shake things up by getting away for a while or breaking out of my usual routine, just like the cows escaping for a few minutes and kicking up their heels in the barnyard. There's nothing wrong with that, but, just as the cows prosper by staying where they belong, I flourish because I'm planted here. Perhaps I've been uprooted so often in my life that now I struggle with the fact that this farm is where I'll live out the rest of my days. Yikes! I must be getting old to be thinking about the end of my life.

Which is better: planted or uprooted? Picture a freshly cut flower, lovingly placed in a vase to adorn the kitchen table. *Look at me! In a place of honor! What a thrill!* But a few days later it's like a scene from *The Wizard of Oz:* "I'm melting, melting." (Yes, my mind takes fabulous leaps every now and then.) So what's my point? Being planted is good.

Back to real life. Now that I've learned the milking routine, my brain is on autopilot while in the milk pit, and that can be dangerous. The constant psht-psst-psht-psst of the pulsator as it harvests the milk from the cows serves as background music, and I escape to distant lands. *Man! I'd rather be anywhere than here,* I silently muse while preparing another cow's udder for the milking machine. *Why didn't I give more consideration to moving closer to my parents before I jumped into this marriage business? I should have just stayed in Charlotte. There was nothing wrong with Charlotte.*

Take another look at the quote that opens this chapter: "Every wakeful step, every mindful act is the direct path to awakening. Wherever you go, there you are." These simple words are overflowing with wisdom for my daily life. Wakeful. Mindful. Alert. Rather than dreaming of distant lands, I should be fully aware of the life going on around me. This is where I'm planted.

The last sentence of Buddha's quote is my favorite: "Wherever you go, there you are." And where am I? In the milk parlor, entertaining inner dreamscapes and the what-ifs of life. The heartbeat of the pulsator continues and woos me back to reality. Weldon is humming an Elvis tune and, out of the blue, remarks, "Mama said there'd be days like this."

For once I was quick with my comeback, "But mama didn't say there'd be sweets like this," and we share a kiss. Magical, real-life moments happen even in the milk pit, and I could have easily missed this one.

God planted me on the farm and he's taking care of me, but the seeds of capricious thoughts will choke out the good stuff. No one knowingly plants weeds. Their seeds are spread by the wind or birds, and they lodge in any little crack of hospitable ground. They grow easily (like weeds!), without any action on our part. And have you ever noticed the roots of those little suckers? If you simply yank off the green part that shows above ground, that ornery thing will pop up again and again. Weeds beget weeds, and that's the way of a restless thought gone haywire. Think. Mull. Think. Brood. Suddenly, a sense of ennui settles over my day. Pretty good parallelism for a non-gardener, don't you think?

Life is complicated. Life is serious business. Blah blah blah. It's time to revive the unhindered spirit of my youth, when the world was my playground and there was no room for boredom. One of my favorite adventures was seeking out a grass-covered, ideally-formed hill. When I found it, I sprinted to the top and surveyed the lay of the land. I lay down, lengthening myself with arms raised over my head, and down the hill I rolled, getting gloriously dizzy. When I came to a stop, I lay there, breathing deeply, gazing into the swirling sky. When the world finally stopped spinning, I'd race back up the hill and do it all over again.

You know, I've never tried rolling down a hill on the farm. The hills have so many rocks, trees, and, quite probably, cow pies. See? There's always an excuse that takes the joy out of life. Maybe I *should* take a walk and look for that perfectly-formed hill. Maybe. I can tell you this for sure: I won't be rolling down it. But I will be keeping my eyes and heart open, looking for opportunities to really live on this chunk of earth called the farm. Since I've been planted here, I'm going to grow and bloom right here. There's certainly enough fertilizer!

Some wise person said, "Boredom is God's way of telling you that you're wasting time."[27] We know that life is work, so let's quit wasting our time dreaming of a better life on the other side of the fence. That field has bugs, ticks, and weeds of its own.

If life is feeling ho-hum, shake it up by changing your attitude, not your locale. Take an honest and thankful look at your life, just as it is. Yank up the weeds that are crowding out the joy. Remember: Wherever you go, there you are. You might as well be there with bells on.

22

A GOD DAY

I will answer them before they even call to me.
While they are still talking about their needs,
I will go ahead and answer their prayers!

~Isaiah 65:24

I'm making a trip to Greensboro," Weldon called out. "Do you want to ride along?"

"Well, sure, if you'll clear a spot in the pickup big enough for my feet and my butt." I grabbed my Kindle, a magazine, a crossword puzzle and a pencil. Instead of taking my purse, I simply fished out a tube of lip gloss and, as an afterthought, grabbed the cell phone. I was ready to go.

What a gorgeous day! Along the interstate, every green thing was vying for attention and the dogwoods were proudly sporting their pink and white blooms. The warm breeze through the open windows did its best to evaporate the drops of perspiration from my forehead, while I secretly wished the air-conditioner worked.

After making our first stop in Greensboro, we continued down the road to the more important task of buying seed corn. After going a few miles, Weldon remarked, "The truck doesn't feel like it's running just right. It seems a little sluggish." A bit later, we both noticed the smell of something hot, and I was pretty sure it wasn't me. Glancing in the rear-view mirror, Weldon saw smoke coming from the back end of the pickup. Luckily, we saw a gas station on our side of the road just a block ahead, so he pulled in and parked in a nicely shaded, out-of-the-way spot.

Checking out the back of the truck, Weldon figured the brakes were dragging on the brake drums. A man was filling a jug with water and pouring it into his radiator, so Weldon called out, "Could I use your container to pour water on the rear brakes of my truck?" While conversing, the guy said he knew a place that could fix the pickup, about a half mile further down the road. He was headed that way and offered to take Weldon there. I gave Weldon the cell phone number in case he needed to call me, but I stayed in the truck, glad to have some time to work on my crossword puzzle.

Soon Weldon called to say he'd be back with a tow truck in about 20 minutes. I had it made in the shade, lazily whiling away the time.

Only later did Weldon tell me this funny story. The guy who took him to the repair shop was in a hurry, so he just let Weldon out on the side of the road, across the street from the repair place. Weldon studied the lay of the land, wondering how he would cross five lanes of rushing traffic. He walked down to the lights, but the crosswalk signals weren't working. Weldon was afraid the next day's headline would read, "Country Bumpkin Run Over on City Street." Looking around, he saw a guy in a truck sitting at the light, so Weldon called out to him, "Are you making a left turn?" *Yes!* "Would you give me a lift around the corner?" *Yes! Hop in!* Who would have thought to ask for a ride (literally) around a corner? And who would have agreed to such a silly request?

Now, back to real time. The tow truck rolled into the gas

station with Weldon in the passenger seat. I joined him there, and we and the pickup were delivered in style to Battleground Tire. We sat in air-conditioned comfort in the waiting room, and, while I made use of a nice clean bathroom, Weldon called his mom to let her know why we weren't home yet. She said Pat had gone to High Point and planned to run a few errands in Greensboro, as well. Mom suggested we call her to see where she was, just in case the truck wasn't easily fixed and we should need a ride home.

While I called Pat, Weldon talked to the mechanic and went to use the facilities. When he came out of the bathroom, I was already off the phone and he asked me where Pat was. I responded, "Across the street." *WHAT?* "Yes, sir." I explained the crazy story to him as I'll explain it to you now.

When I reached her on the phone, Pat asked me where we were. I gave her the name of the business, the address on Battleground Avenue, and told her I could see Lowe's Home Improvement across the street.

She said, "*I'm* on Battleground Avenue." Then, in her usual style, she told me the names of all the streets she had taken instead of her usual, straightforward route from High Point to Greensboro. "I stopped at Starbucks just a few minutes ago," she continued, "but when my phone rang, I pulled into the CVS parking lot where I'm sitting now. Hey! I can see a Lowe's from here. Is the building you're in blue?" I answered with a resounding *Yes!* Then she blurted out, "I'm across the street from you!" If her story doesn't make sense to you, don't worry. It didn't make sense to me, either. All that mattered was her last exclamation: "I'm across the street from you!"

The woman behind the counter heard me telling Weldon this wild story. She said, "And some people say there isn't a God." Then in walked Pat. As she related the story to a few more people, we were advised that the truck would be ready around noon the next day. We piled into Pat's vehicle and headed home.

Passing through Winston-Salem, Weldon asked if we could stop at Krispy Kreme. "I think I deserve a doughnut after this crazy day." Pat and I stayed in the car while he went inside.

Surprisingly, he came back out and asked if we'd like an ice cream cone. Of course we would. Then he said, "This morning I dreamed of a chocolate ice cream cone, and now my dream has come true."

Throughout this day, never once did I grumble or even think about grumbling. I never fumed, *Man! What a waste of a good day. Think of all the stuff I could have accomplished today.* That, in and of itself, was a miracle.

In the dark of night, before dozing off, Weldon said, "You were praying, weren't you?"

"Uh, no, I don't think so. I suppose I sent up a prayer or two, but nothing frantic."

"You know," he said, "it seemed like everything fell into place before we even had time to pray about it."

Every day is a God day, of course, but today was more other-worldly than usual. We are amazed and thankful. Sweet dreams.

23

HELP IS ON THE WAY

Life doesn't make any sense without interdependence.
We need each other, and the sooner we learn that,
the better for us all.

~Joan (Mrs. Erik) Erikson[28]

On our wedding day, Weldon was cutting corn up until two hours before the ceremony began. It turns out that a perfect day for a wedding in September is also a perfect day for harvesting corn. I didn't know it then, but I surely know it now: Cutting and chopping corn is the biggest event of the year on the dairy farm, because chopped corn (aka silage) is the mainstay of the milk cows' diet. A little thing like a wedding mustn't get in the way.

Weldon is known near and far as the best corn grower in the area. People stop by just to see how his crop is coming along. In his own estimation, the crop is never quite as good as it could be and never measures up to what he grew twelve or thirteen years ago. He has a dried corn stalk from that year lying in the hay mow that measures nineteen-and-a-half feet tall. I think he should have had it bronzed.

Because bringing in the corn is such a big and important job, Mr. I-Can-Handle-It-Myself actually calls on a few friends or neighbors for help. Typically, Weldon drives the tractor that pulls the chopper, a willing helper drives the tractor and wagon that receives the chopped corn, and another friend runs the machine that blows the chopped corn into the silo. My participation consists of cooking a big lunch for the guys and documenting the event with my camera. This is the stuff that fuels romantic images of life on the farm.

The farm has been in the family since 1804 and has been a dairy farm since the early 1930s. Other than driving a school bus while he was in high school, working on the farm has been Weldon's only employment. He and his dad worked side-by-side for 32 years and never hired outside help. Although it started out as a two-man family business, it's now a one-man enterprise.

I have often puzzled over this "family farm" conundrum: Why did Wendell and Edith have just one son? Why didn't Weldon and his first wife have any sons? Surely God knew that able-bodied men are needed to handle the heavy work of farming. My questions were answered one evening when our friend Papa John brought a group of 4H-ers and their parents to the farm at milking time. One of the parents asked Weldon, "What do you do with the calves?"

Weldon replied, "We keep the females and sell the males. There's no need for males on a dairy farm."

It was a light bulb moment: No need for males on a dairy farm. Weldon should thank the good Lord above that his father hadn't totally subscribed to that precept.

Now, where was I? Oh, yes: the fact that Weldon is the man on this one-man farm and he rarely calls on anyone for help.

Friday morning, Weldon made the passing comment, "I think I might be coming down with something. There's a tickle in the back of my throat." On Saturday, he confirmed he was feeling lousy with a headache and congestion. A little cold or, for that matter, even a big cold, can't stop a farmer. I remember only one time in our years together when Weldon said, "You'd better call around and see if you can find someone to help me with chores." This was not that time.

We did chores on Sunday morning but, not wanting to spread his germs around, Weldon stayed home from church. During the service, I asked for prayer that Weldon would get over the crud quickly, because a farmer can't take a day off to rest and get all better. That afternoon, Alton (a friend from church) called. "What time will Weldon start chores? A few of us guys will come by to help with milking."

While eating supper that evening, Todd (another friend from church) knocked on the door. "Come in. Pull up a chair and have supper with us," Weldon said. That's what he always says, even when, as in this case, we're eating the last of the leftovers and there's nothing else hiding in the fridge. I was ready to pray for a recurrence of the loaves and fishes miracle, but Todd said he had already eaten.

"No, I don't need a thing. I'm here to help with chores," he said. He joined us at the table and chatted as we finished our meal. Then Weldon and Todd went out and I did the dishes. I changed into my milk duds and got the cat food ready.

After feeding the cats and kittens and watching them tussle for their fair share of the tender morsels, I continued on to the calf shed. I was surprised how quiet it was. The young ones are usually maa-ing and bert-ing, rattling the gates and chains while they eagerly anticipate their warm, bottled milk. "What? Have they been fed already?" Since I couldn't answer myself with any certainty, I sauntered on to the milk barn.

I opened the door and had difficulty finding an empty square of floor for my feet. Weldon was at the far wall, getting the milking system ready. Pat was rinsing soapy milk bottles at the sink, and five guys from church were talking, laughing, and carrying on as they worked. One was scrubbing the last of the milk bottles, two were soaping up buckets, one was rinsing the buckets with the water hose, and the youngest was cavorting with all the cats and kittens underfoot.

What a blessing! After talking with the guys and thanking

them profusely, I was able to go home…without helping with the milking and without the least bit of guilt.

Except during the corn harvest, Weldon rarely asks anyone (outside the family) for help. I tend to be the same way. *I can handle this, no problem. And if it is a problem, it's my problem.* Our self-sufficiency isolates us.

Has farming always been such a one-man show? I've read about the good old days of barn raisings, quilting bees, and hog slaughtering. The good old days? Quilting, maybe, but you can keep the rest. Anyway, neighbor helped neighbor, knowing that the favor would be returned. Now, at least in this area, farms are few and far between, crowded out by cities populated with independent people.

I remember the days of knowing our neighbors, stopping by for a friendly hello, or nonchalantly walking over to borrow an egg or a cup of sugar. In today's world, too often it's only the most desperate straits that send us running to a neighbor for help.

Why is it so hard to admit that we need other people every now and then? We're taught to be strong, put on a happy face, and live with a can-do attitude. There's nothing wrong with doing our best, but how wonderfully right it is to ask for and accept a helping hand or, just as important, a listening ear.

Just as we need each other, we need God. We are loathe to ask people for help and we are often slow to ask for God's help. Some say that God is a crutch, but anyone who has a broken leg is glad for the assistance a crutch provides—and our lives are broken, aren't they?

Over and over again, the Bible tells us that God is here to help us, but we're so proud. Who needs God! This reminds me of a conversation I had with my brother Ricky shortly after I became a Christian. He said, "You seem different. What's up?" I was taken aback, because I didn't think trusting in God's love and care would show on the outside. I mean, I was already a really nice person. I explained that I had entrusted my life into God's care.

Now it was Rick's turn to be surprised. "But, why? I

thought that was for drunks lying in a gutter. Why would you need God?" (He didn't need to clarify that he put me in the goody-two-shoes category.) We had a long conversation and, after explaining that everyone needs God in this life and for the next, I prayed with him that he would recognize his own need and put his life into God's hands, too.

God made us to be capable, hard-working people, but balance is a beautiful thing. Standing on our own and leaning on others. Helping and being helped. Giving and receiving.

Our lives are enriched when we recognize our weakness and ask for help. We need each other. We need the Lord.

24

HUFFING AND PUFFING

Old age ain't no place for sissies.

~Bette Davis[29]

After seeing just a small portion of all that Weldon does on the farm, visitors exclaim, "Dairy farming is such hard work!" And, without fail, Weldon replies, "It's not *hard* work, it's just 24/7 nonstop work." That's the truth as he sees it, after a lifetime on the dairy farm.

Here's how I see it: Dairy farming is crazy hard work. More precisely, dairy farming on a one-man dairy farm is crazy hard work. And, since one man really can't do it all by himself, the chores are time-consuming and exhausting for the old ladies who come alongside to help.

Over the years, I've learned to help where I can, except for building a fire in the milk parlor's wood stove during the cold months. I left that chore to Weldon. As it turns out, it was his mom who built the fire, and that rankled me no end. When she could no longer help with chores, Pat started making the fires. I don't understand how Weldon can leave this job for women who are older than he, but that's a slough I no longer wallow in. I will add, however, that I rarely build a fire in the wood stove at home, either. If he sees I can build a fire, I'm certain he'll quietly relegate that job to me. End of ranting.

After mastering the art of milking cows, it was only logical that I learn how to help care for the calves. The babies aren't left with their moms beyond the first day because the dairy farmer needs to put the mom into the milking rotation. In this line of work, it's the milk that brings in the money. Calves are put in the calf shed and mom can touch noses with her youngster through the gate. A new mom's milk is milked into a separate pail, put into a bottle, and fed to her calf for a few days to build up the baby's immunity. Each "season" starts with just one calf, but we'll soon be bottle-feeding eight or ten young ones. By the time they're three weeks old, they're nibbling hay. Soon they eat feed pellets and learn to drink from a small bucket held under their noses. It sounds so sweet. Just wait till you're holding that bucket for them and they give it a good hard butt with their nose...right into your leg or belly. Youch! Not nearly so sweet.

When they're young, they're cute and I laugh as they kick up their heels and race from one end of the shed to the other. Pat names them all and takes good care of them. Almost from the start, they weigh more than I do and, consequently, I don't trust the little buggers. If they get loose from their chains or ropes, I can't catch them or tie them, so I stay away and call for Weldon. Pat is stronger and braver than I, but there comes a time when they're too big and frisky even for her. I'll just stick with the kitties.

Between four and six months old, calves (now more accurately called young heifers) are weaned and they begin to eat silage. Pat and I stand at the feeding trough and scoop silage by hand into five-gallon buckets. Eeuuww. Feels gross, smells worse. Who knew I was such a girlie girl? Honestly, I rarely helped fill the buckets. But, not to be outdone by Pat, I gritted my teeth, flexed my muscles, and tried my hand (and arms and neck and back) at carrying five-gallon buckets of silage. I was convinced that I'd get stronger as I lugged those heavy buckets to the heifer shed, but oh the aches and pains! We smartened up a bit and used a little red wagon to help with the toting, but there was still the job of lifting the filled buckets up and into the wagon. Hundred-and-ten-pound weakling that I am, it wasn't long before I wisely bowed out of chores that required heavy lifting or carrying.

Mysteriously, magically, over the span of four or five years, my milking chores stretched into five, then six, and, occasionally, even seven hours a day. There were always additional tasks that needed doing, and I tried my best to be a good little helper. Although my early "farm assist" years included two days off during the week, the pressure of never-ending opportunities for work caused my weekend (usually Monday and Tuesday) to fall by the wayside. I was now tired and cranky most of the time, and I had aches and pains in places I didn't know I had.

If milking cows were my only job, I suppose I could have continued. However, I was still determined to keep the house neat and clean, and if I didn't cook the meals, we wouldn't eat. A woman's work is never done, a farmer's work is never done, and I was trying to excel at both.

Huffing and puffing because I was toting buckets of silage that were too heavy for me was understandable. But now, due to physical exhaustion (which I wasn't acknowledging), I was sighing and humphing over life in general, sporting quite the negative attitude. *Life is so hard. Poor me. Waanh, waanh, waanh.* I was turning into a grumpy old woman.

I finally realized that I was plumb tuckered and worn out. The first thing I did was reclaim my two days off each week. There was no sense in feeling bad about it; I had to take care of myself. I also discovered that, although I don't nap (that is, *sleep* briefly during the day), lying down for ten or fifteen minutes was a refreshing break that enabled me to make it through the rest of the day. What a wonderful revelation.

I'm not a spring chicken anymore, so it's important to recognize that my body and my needs may be changing. Whining about the changes or feeling guilty about them doesn't make any sense and doesn't make life any easier. The phrase "know thyself" comes to mind, and knowing oneself is an ongoing process. I'm not the same person I was 30 years ago or maybe even 30 months ago. People all around me are changing and I don't think it's weird or hold it against them. I'm learning to give myself the same freedom.

Remember Weldon's confident statement in the opening paragraph about dairy farming not being hard? Now, a decade later, this is what he says: "Is this farm work getting harder, or am I just getting older?"

It happens to the best of us.

25
YOU-NIQUE

It takes courage to grow up and become who you really are.

~e.e. cummings[30]

Weldon and I had been married for many years before someone had the guts to say aloud what many had been thinking: "She's a city girl, he's a country boy. How will this ever work?" Now, sitting beside me at a potluck supper, Gail chuckled after admitting her early misgivings. She quickly went on to say she was glad things had worked out for us, because everyone loved Weldon and wanted the best for him. Then she opened her purse and pulled out photos of her uncle, proudly exclaiming, "Weldon looks like him, doesn't he? They're both skinny as a rail and quite similar in demeanor: so kind, hard working, and gentle." I smiled at her honest admission of concern and felt a bond of kinship as she gave me a peek into her own life.

I didn't see myself as a city girl, but Gail's words stirred the memory pot. Through second grade, I lived in a tiny dot on the map called Kettle River, Minnesota. We took a step up on the population scale when we moved to Cambridge, Minnesota, where I finished my elementary and high school education. Fresh out of high school, my young husband and I almost experienced city living by moving to the suburbs of Minneapolis/St. Paul. Next stop: Brimson, Minnesota. With just a one-stop bar and convenience store where you could buy a gallon of milk that tasted like cigarette smoke, I'm still not convinced it could actually be called a town. From there, we moved to a rural setting in Haiti.

When I was 42 years old, I left Haiti (and my husband) and nestled into a quiet residential area of Charlotte, North Carolina. Although cultural events, fancy dining, and bustling nightlife were easily accessible, they held no attraction for me. I did, however, start wearing makeup, had my hair cut by a professional (rather than hacking it off myself in the bathroom), and owned a number of decent business suits. I wasn't part of the elite crowd, but I took small, hopeful steps to leave Dorkville behind. Perhaps ten years of working in the city *had* changed me.

Now, here I am, back in Small Town, USA, living on a dairy farm. "You ain't from around here, are you?" People in Charlotte rarely mentioned my Minnesotan accent, but here everyone knows that I'm not home folk. I'm painfully aware of that fact, too, when Weldon finishes chatting with a friend and I have to ask, "What did he say?" I definitely ain't from around here.

Also, everyone is related to everyone else. Large, extended families are the norm, and they all live along the same road or right around the corner. Okay, I'm exaggerating a little, but it seems like everyone knows everyone else. It's too much to keep straight in my head.

Southern people are really friendly, and rural southerners are even friendlier. Previous to moving to the farm, I never knew people could talk so much and in such detail. It might be because I'm from Minnesota. Maybe it's because of my Finnish heritage. Whatever the reason, I can relate to *Dragnet's* Joe Friday[31] and his

"Just the facts, ma'am. Just the facts."

My reactions to this strange new world have surprised and dismayed me, prompting me to ask, *What is the matter with me?* As it turns out, nothing is the matter with me. I'm just me, but it's taken a lot of years to recognize who I am and not feel like I have to fit into some preconceived picture of what a person/wife/mother/friend should look like. At the same time, life on the farm pushes me to be more than who I think I am. Does that make sense? Let me give you a few examples.

Early in life, I knew I didn't want to be a nurse. My response to any ailment is, "Take two aspirins and don't call me in the morning." Unfortunately, the farm's cats and kittens get sick or injured, and an aspirin isn't going to help them. With tears in my eyes, I call on Weldon to make everything all better. Over the years, believe it or not, I've acquired skills to help keep our cats healthier and I can play doctor when needed.

Learning to milk cows was one thing. The process revealed that I'm a willing student and a good helper. Milking cows and participating in the related chores morning and evening, five, six, or seven days a week for six years was another thing. Now I boldly proclaim, "I'm not a dairymaid."

Spring and summer on the farm include gardening. Am I a gardener? No way! I've told my daughters, "It's a good thing you are girls. Had you been plants, you'd be dead by now." But how can I possibly sit in the house while Edith, Pat, and Beth are sweating in the garden? Of course I join in, picking up rocks, making straight rows, planting seeds, pulling weeds, and harvesting the vegetables. I love Edith's gentle hinting: "There are plenty of green beans and tomatoes in the garden, if you need any." No, I don't enjoy gardening, but I do love the end results.

Because Weldon and his family love me completely and unconditionally, I'm getting to know myself better. Knowing who we are is important, but there can still be times when we don't measure up to our own high standards. I'll never measure up to the women in this family, but what a relief to realize no one is asking me to change. If God loves me (idiosyncrasies, foibles, and all), shouldn't I accept myself?

Colossians 3:23 says we should do everything wholeheartedly, as though we're doing it for the Lord. I would also add, we should wholeheartedly be ourselves, remembering that labels don't make us who we are. I'm not a southern belle, but I have good manners and I'll gladly listen to your stories. I'm not a milk maid, but I'm a pretty good helper. I'm not a gardener, but every now and then something I plant actually grows. I'm not a nurse, but I won't leave you lying and dying on the floor. Even when we're asked to do tasks out of our comfort zone, outside our area of expertise, let's do it with enthusiasm. In the process, we're growing and becoming who we really are.

God has made each of us unique. We should only compare ourselves with ourselves. "Am I the best me I can be? Am I living in a way that pleases the God who made me?" The prison doors are thrown open when we realize that God made me ME and God made you YOU. Emulating someone we admire is fine, but let's shine at being who we are. We each have gifts, abilities, quirks, and hidden treasures within us. Let's nurture them and use them to full advantage.

You have a role, a destiny, a dream to fulfill in this world, so do it in your own cool-and-calm or wild-and-wacky way. And remember to take a bow every now and then.

26

AN ANGRY MOMENT

Human anger does not produce the righteousness God desires.

~James 1:20

How can a morning go so wrong so quickly? I rinsed the pre-breakfast dishes, washed down the counter tops, and started to get the cat food ready. Weldon was at the front door, putting on his jacket, about to head out to morning chores. "I watered this plant the other day," he said, pointing to the one and only plant in the front room.

"Yes, I watered it a few days ago, too," I replied.

"It looks pretty dry," he continued. Then, there he was at the sink, dumping the ornamental rocks and shells from around the little plastic pot into an empty cup, a handful of them falling to the floor. "Oops. I'm making a mess."

"Yes, you are. Give it to me. I'll finish it." So, I take the pot from him and give the plant a gulp of water. Then he asks me if the big plant in the living room is still alive, and off he goes to check it out.

Suddenly I'm fuming, because growing plants is not my forte and he knows it. Just what was he trying to prove? When he came back to the front room he made a comment that, due to the steam puffing out of my ears, I didn't fully catch. But I do remember my reply to him: "Just mind your own damn business!" Yup, that's what I said.

Weldon calmly went out to start his morning chores while I, growling and scowling, finished arranging the rocks and shells around the now well-watered green troublemaker. I got the cat food ready and took it out to the cats. Then, after the calves were fed, I found Weldon in the milk parlor and interrupted his work. "I'm sorry for what I said this morning."

"Oh, don't worry about it. It was nothing."

To me, it *was* something—an angry outburst, completely out of character for me. I wish I had obeyed the exhortation from my childhood: *If you can't say something nice, don't say anything at all.* Or called to mind a verse that I actually know by heart: *May the words of my mouth and the meditation of my heart be pleasing to you, O LORD, my rock and my redeemer.* (Psalm 19:14)

Now, here I sit, pounding out my therapy on the keyboard and burning Weldon's breakfast sausage at the same time. This is *exactly* how a morning can go so wrong so quickly.

● ● ●

P.S. The next morning we both chuckled over the plant-watering debacle. The case was firmly closed when Weldon said, "Don't worry. I'm gonna mind my own damn business!" I laughed out loud. And I kept laughing through the chores, the wind and rain, the thunder and lightning, and the mud. Ahh, what a difference a day makes.

The moral of the story: Even when I get my undies in a bundle, it's good to keep my mouth shut and remember that this, too, shall pass.

27

THE GREATEST OF THESE

For one human being to love another: that is perhaps the most difficult of all our tasks, the ultimate, the last test and proof, the work for which all other work is but preparation.

~Rainer Maria Rilke[32]

While we were dating, Weldon and I often went out to eat on the Saturday or Sunday that we spent together. We'd go to a fast-food restaurant, where he ordered a simple hamburger (lettuce and tomato only, please) and fries. Another favorite was going to a buffet, where he loaded his plate with meats and veggies and plenty of bread and desserts. Weldon has simple tastes when it comes to food: nothing too spicy; nothing with cheese, sour cream, or cream cheese; and nothing mushy, except for mashed potatoes. And please don't jumble everything up in a hot dish or casserole. He prefers good, old-fashioned home cooking.

For the farmer, eating out is about sustenance; for me, it's about the experience (and not having to cook, set the table, serve the food, clear the table, wash the dishes, and put everything away). I made a deal with Weldon before we got married: "We have to go out to eat once a month to keep my taste buds happy and to introduce you to a greater variety of foods." I didn't think I was asking too much, but soon I realized that going out to eat with Weldon wasn't a treat. Restaurants are too loud, the food too salty, and the inevitable question is always asked, "Do we get bread with this?" I felt like the biggest loser in this deal, but I couldn't, in good conscience, hold Weldon to our premarital agreement.

On a sun-dappled drive to church, Weldon surprised me by asking if I'd like to go out for lunch. "Well, sure!" He didn't say anything else, but I guessed we'd head to one of the little restaurants in King or maybe the buffet in Mount Airy.

After church, we got in the car and he started driving to … I didn't know where. *Ah, I bet it's the seafood place in Rural Hall.* But, no, he pulled into the parking lot of a Mexican restaurant. Well, blow me down. We walked in, the hostess seated us, and I (still in shock) helped Weldon search the menu for an entree he might enjoy. When the waitress came, he ordered a steak, without the cheese and without the strange-sounding sauce. Once more: No cheese. No sauce. "I'm just a plain-kind-of guy," Weldon said.

The meal and our time together were both gratifying. I mentally labeled this surreal event a miracle. He didn't go to the restaurant for his sake, but specifically to please me.

While we were dating, Weldon sent me flowers at work, once for my birthday and once for no special reason. Not long after the marriage vows, reality (also known as end-of-courtship) stuck its nose into the idyllic landscape. Having a gorgeous bouquet of flowers delivered, or even purchasing flowers from the florist and hand delivering them is pretty pricey. So what does Weldon do? When he's out in the fields on his tractor, in the middle of a hard day of work, he stops what he's doing, picks a bouquet of wildflowers, and brings them home to me. His mom, with a proud smile on her face, says, "From the time he could toddle around, he would pick flowers and bring them in for me."

A few years ago, we went to an office supply store to purchase receipt books for the business of farming. Being a little headache-y and tired, I moseyed over to the office chairs. It felt good to sit down. Then I plopped myself in another chair and then another. When Weldon found me, I exclaimed, "Try out these chairs. They're so comfortable. That one over there looks just right for you." Like unruly children, we hopped from one chair to the next, but one in particular kept calling my name.

"If you like it, get it," Weldon said. "I'll buy it for you."

"No, I don't need a new chair. I'm just enjoying myself."

"But you're going to be writing a book. You need a good chair." What? I didn't think he was listening when I spoke of my serious plans to write. Is it possible he hears even when he doesn't make any sort of response? Anyway, I hadn't been thinking of a new chair, and it was a spur-of-the-moment decision I couldn't make. The receipt books were wrapped in a bag, my heart was cloaked in love, and we went home.

What is it that holds me to this farm...this farm that is the butt end of my complaints? Love. Not love for the farm, but love for Weldon. It's not an ooey-gooey feeling, but a commitment to share my life with him. I can talk about love all day long, but if I don't do anything that demonstrates my love, it's not love at all.

The Bible says God *is* love and he is rich in kindness. *Rich* in kindness! Romans 2:4 brings it down to the nitty-gritty: "Don't you see how wonderfully kind, tolerant, and patient God is with you? Does this mean nothing to you? Can't you see that his kindness is intended to turn you from your sin?"

Kindness is the offspring of love, and love is the only measure, the only motivation that lasts for the long haul. (The long haul. Hauling manure. My brain follows strange paths after all these years on the farm. I definitely prefer to haul love and kindness rather than manure.) Since God is kind and patient (wonderfully kind and patient!), I should be kind and patient with Weldon. Day after day after day. In spite of my inner grumblings, it's love for Weldon and his family that inspires me to help around the farm. After all, love is an action verb.

Besides helping with chores, how do I demonstrate kindness and love to Weldon? What am I doing just for him, to show him that I think he's special and important? I listen attentively to his long and detailed accounts of how a machine works, why a particular job is done the way it's done, and how this person I don't know is related to the lady who died yesterday, whom I also don't know. When he's finished, I may not fully understand what he was talking about or have any clue as to who this dead person is, but he knows I'm interested in the things that matter to him.

The way to a man's heart is through his stomach. I know it's a cliche, but it's true for Weldon. I cook meals he enjoys and appreciates. When I make a trip to Winston-Salem, I often swing by Krispy Kreme to pick up doughnuts for him, and I make sure the cookie jar is well-stocked. A black raspberry pie, fresh from the oven, puts a grin on his face that stretches from one ear to the other. He's so easy.

While slogging through the mud after a heavy rain, or when I slip and slide on the poo as I make my way through the calf shed to feed the babies, I should whisper to myself, "I'm doing this because of love." Whew! Living and loving can wear you plumb out.

I'll end these reflections with some powerful words from 1 Corinthians 13, known as the "love chapter" in the Bible.

"Love is patient and kind. Love is not jealous or boastful or proud or rude. It does not demand its own way. It is not irritable, and it keeps no record of being wronged. It does not rejoice about injustice but rejoices whenever the truth wins out. Love never gives up, never loses faith, is always hopeful, and endures through every circumstance. Three things last forever—faith, hope, and love—and the greatest of these is love."

28

JUST SAY NO

Didn't you hear me? I am busy!
Sweet Baby Jesus, have mercy on my soul!

~Scott Dannemiller[33]

There are things I can't do and, every once in a while, things I *won't* do. Take the time Weldon was standing in the front yard and hollering, "Get out the pot!" I hurriedly opened the door to see what all the commotion was about. There he stood, holding up a huge snapping turtle by its tail. "Turtle soup!" he exclaimed.

Uhm, no. That I *won't* do. Fortunately, he was kidding... but I wasn't. No way was I going to attempt turtle stew or turtle *anything*. If I had said, "Great! A quick search on the Internet and I'll get right on it," he would have been tickled and I would have been stuck. But I was bold enough to say, "No way!" It does make a great story, though.

Two-and-a-half weeks before my 62nd birthday, Weldon

and I were in the middle of milking and we started tossing around words like sabbatical, vacation, leave of absence, and retirement. Weldon was dreaming of vacation, but my mind traveled a different path. *Retire.* The word was a tender morsel on my tongue and, after savoring it for a few minutes I said, "I think I'll retire on my birthday." Weldon grunted.

Over the next few days, one or the other of us would make a passing reference to retirement. Wanting to reassure him, I clarified, "I'm just speaking of retiring from milking cows, you know. I'll continue to cook and clean and care for you." Weldon snorted.

Retirement was now a living, breathing entity. Whether sweet, ferocious, or wheedling, I could hear the words, "You can retire. Just say *no* to cows."

My birthday arrived without fanfare and, as usual, I started the day in the living room with a cup of coffee and my Bible. In the kitchen, Weldon finished his orange juice, opened the door, and called to me, "I'm going out."

"Okay, I'll be there shortly." And, I was. We had milked a few cows when, as though seeing me for the first time, Weldon exclaimed, "I thought you were going to retire."

"Well, I feel a tinge of guilt. I can't do it quite yet." I'm such a wimp. We finished our chores, returned to the house, scarfed down breakfast, and got ready for church.

Ten days later, again during morning chores, I looked at Weldon and simply said, "I can't do this any more." And that was that. I retired from cows.

Surprisingly, I didn't feel too guilty about it. Most of me was simply exhausted, but a little piece of me hoped that Weldon would see that he couldn't continue doing this "farm thing" forever. As long as we old ladies kept helping him, he could keep milking cows. Now, he had one less helper.

I still feed the cats, of course, and when calves are bottle fed, I help with that. However, when I found out that Pat was not only doing all the stuff she usually did, but was also washing down the milk parlor after milking (a job I used to do), I felt bad. Really bad. She doesn't help with the actual milking, but she does everything else. A year after my retirement, she's putting in six-hour days, seven days a week, and that doesn't include all of the church and community things she does. She could write a book.

After doing my measly little chores, when I'm ready to head back to the house, I make a point to thank Pat for all she does. The day she responded with "I'm glad to do it," my mouth dropped open in amazement.

"What? Don't say that. You make me feel like a bum."

"It's the family farm, and I feel like it's my duty to do whatever I can to help my brother. Really, it's okay."

Ouch. I still feel lower than a snake's belly, but I silently defend my action (or, more precisely, my inaction) by thinking, *Well, it's not my farm. And Pat could just say no.* Oh my. Why does life feel so complicated?

I no longer milk cows but life is as busy as ever and, yes, frustrations and aggravations still make house calls. I don't get stuff done that needs doing or finish projects that I started long ago.

The biblical story of Mary and Martha comes to mind. Jesus hadn't phoned ahead to let them know he was coming, but Martha knew exactly what to do when he knocked on the door. She gave him a hug, led him to the most comfortable chair, fluffed the pillows, and headed to the kitchen. I imagine her thinking, "Oh, no! Just a few leftovers in the fridge. I'll run to the store and pick up a few things, and then I'll whip up a yummy meal for our special guest. Jesus deserves the best." And that's exactly what she does.

What was her sister Mary doing all this while? She was sitting in the living room, listening to the stories Jesus was telling, hanging on his every word.

Martha bustles into the living room in a huff, the dish towel thrown over her shoulder. "Jesus! Tell Mary to get into the kitchen and help me. I can't believe she's just sitting here while I do all the work. She's such a slacker."

Jesus responded, "Martha, Martha. You're so uptight, so riled up over your housework and chores. The most important thing in life is spending time with God and his people. That's what Mary has chosen, and no one can take that away from her."

I admit, I'm taking a little poetic license with the story. You can read the real deal in Luke 10, verses 38 to 42.

So how is my life since retirement? Do, do, do. Work, work, work. Hurry, hurry, hurry. I picture Jesus saying, "Cindy, Cindy. Didn't you retire from your busyness? You don't have to do everything today. Chill out. Take time to smell the roses. Oh, that's right, you don't have any roses. Sit down. Read. Call your daughters. Go visit Mom Edith."

We can retire from our place of employment, but we can't retire from life. Okay, we'll all retire from this life one day, but that's a whole 'nother story. We *can* retire from our busyness —we *must* retire from our busyness, because it's ruining our lives.

Scott Dannemiller (quoted at the beginning of this chapter) writes a blog called *The Accidental Missionary*. In a post titled "Busy Is a Sickness," he described his crazy busy day to a friend. His friend's response surprised both the author of the blog and me: "Sounds like a full day. Have fun!"

Our attitude sets the stage. If Martha had been preparing lunch for Jesus because that's what she really wanted to do, she would have been humming a happy tune in the midst of her busyness. Instead, she was boiling as furiously as the water kettle on the stove. Mary was busy, too, but it was a peaceful busy, visiting with her friend.

Look over your daily planner. See which events can be deleted, which events need to receive a resounding *No!* Then go through your day spouting this satisfying mantra: "I have a full day! It's all good."

29

HIDDEN BLESSINGS

*Search your problems, and within them you will discover the
well-disguised mercies of God.*

~Ray Pritchard[34]

A t the tender age of 18, I married my high school
sweetheart. Five years later, I gave birth to my first
daughter, and three years after that, my second daughter.
Being a mother was (and continues to be) my favorite pastime.
When I was 30 years old, this little family of four moved to Haiti,
and I gave myself wholly to interacting with the local people in a
meaningful way.

Like coffee forgotten in the pot, marital troubles had
been brewing for years. We were masters of disguise but, after
almost 25 years of marriage, my husband and I divorced. From
Haiti, I moved to Charlotte and learned how to live on my own
for the first time in my life. How's that for wrapping up 30 years
of my life in two succinct paragraphs?

At the not-so-tender age of 53, along with getting to know my new husband and his family, I found myself living in what appeared to be an alternate universe. Welcome to the farm, indeed. Now, where did I put those rose-colored glasses?

On the outside, I made a good show of adapting to my new reality. However, as you've already seen, over the years my happy-go-lucky path took a downward turn. Life was full of pitfalls and hidden snares that tripped me up and made me snarl. Questions fomented like a witch's concoction. What's wrong with me? Why do I have such a bad attitude? Where are these negative thoughts coming from, and why won't they leave me alone?

The most obvious answer to my brooding questions is simply admitting that life is difficult, but I'm a master at pretending and "put on a happy face" has always been my motto. Unfortunately, it's hard to keep up appearances while huddled in a woe-is-me corner. I wanted a better answer.

Socrates[35] said, "The unexamined life is not worth living." That seems pretty harsh. However, now that I'm retired from cows, I decide it's time to get up, dust off my rear end, and do just that. Thanks to this book, you're now privy to my inner musings and many of the struggles and adjustments I've been through in the last ten years. You're welcome.

A whisper of wisdom riffles across my heart when I hear Laura Story's song, Blessings.[36] In it, she says we pray for all the things that make life rosy and comfortable. Then she poses some hard questions: What if our struggles and tears are actually a means of blessing? What if we see God more clearly after wrestling with the perplexities of life?

If nothing else, my years in this crazy farm world have shown me that I'm not as cheerful and perfect as I imagined myself to be. And I don't need to pretend that everything is hunky-dory all the time. If the difficulties are teaching me about real life, honesty, and God's mercy, they really are blessings, aren't they?

Examining my life continued via the book of Ecclesiastes during our ladies' Bible study. In Ecclesiastes 5:19 and 20, Solomon (touted to be the wisest man in the world) says, "It is a good thing to receive wealth from God and the good health to enjoy it. To enjoy your work and accept your lot in life—this is indeed a gift from God. God keeps such people so busy enjoying life that they take no time to brood over the past."

I believe the Bible is a book that is "alive." God speaks to us personally through his book, if we're willing to listen. What we hear may not be exactly what the scholars say it means, but we get a message that fits our personal situation, right where we are. I felt like God was talking to me in these verses, so I read and reread them in various translations, trying to see how they related to my own experiences. My gleanings follow.

All through my years, I've felt blessed and wealthy. ("It is a good thing to receive wealth from God.") The wealth wasn't in money but in a sense of fulfillment provided by each chapter of my life. I've enjoyed my work as a wife, mother, homemaker, teacher, and missionary. Actively enjoying life didn't leave much time for brooding.

After leaving my first husband and moving to Charlotte, I made mistakes and struggled to find my way. But as the Lord got me back on solid ground, my life and work once again became joyful. God was keeping me "occupied with the gladness" of my heart (as the New American Standard version puts it).

Then it was on to the dairy farm. Life was new and vibrant with a funny, attentive husband, a loving family close at hand, and kitties topping it all off like fluffy frosting on a cake. A house longing to be transformed into a home called for none other than Susie Homemaker, and she rolled up her sleeves with gusto.

Then...barn chores. I worked willingly and with all my heart, intent on being the best little milkmaid ever. But the yuck and the grunge were a constant irritation. I was incessantly wiping, washing, wanting things to be clean and orderly. Morning milk chores, mid-day house chores, evening milk chores. Day after day, every day. The more work I did outside, the less work I did inside; the more tired my body, the more discouraged my spirit.

Rather than enjoying this new way of living, I started

mulling over the years of my life. I continued to help with the chores, but at the same time, I was stewing over the mess I was in and the mess I was becoming. And let me confess right here: Susie Homemaker couldn't take it either. She packed her bags and left just a few days ago.

The verses from Ecclesiastes propose just one good solution: Rejoice in the work at hand and see it as a gift from God. When we're happy in our work, we aren't fretting about life; we're enjoying it. Although I did my best to put a good face on it, I was *not* happy in my work. I tried. Really, I tried!

If I had seen these verses before retiring from cows, would I have miraculously become glad in my work? Gritting my teeth, doing my best, and putting on my sunshine face helped a little. Praying and doing every good "Christian thing" I knew to do helped a little more. But what really did the trick was walking out of the milk barn. Admitting defeat? Giving up? Call it what you will, I'm definitely back to enjoying life.

Another truth is that time and space reveal a different perspective. Life wasn't perfect in Northern Minnesota or in Haiti or in Charlotte, but I look back fondly on those years. Now I see lessons learned through divorce and the false steps I took while getting back on my feet. I'm glad I helped with farm chores. I have a new respect for all people who work the land and tend animals and try to keep a clean house in spite of it all. Plus, I'm writing a book to help me sort through the mess.

Life isn't always easy, but if you find yourself brooding and unhappy with what's right in front of you, take time to scrutinize your longings and actions. By making small changes, could you get back to enjoying your work and your place in this world? Is God making you thirst for something only He can provide, so that you will turn to him? Go ahead. Examine your life—how it is, how it was, and even how you wish it could be. Look for the blessings hidden in the daily routine and frustrations. Ask God to give you new eyes and a new perspective.

"To enjoy your work and accept your lot in life—this is indeed a gift from God."

30

THE MIRACLE DRUG

Gratitude unlocks the fullness of life. It turns what we have into enough, and more. It turns denial into acceptance, chaos to order, confusion to clarity. It can turn a meal into a feast, a house into a home, a stranger into a friend. Gratitude makes sense of our past, brings peace for today, and creates a vision for tomorrow.

~Melody Beattie[37]

W ithout fail, Thanksgiving Day finds me calling my daughters. They expect my call, I'm sure, but they don't know when it will happen. With the advent of the "smart" phone, they know I'm on the other end of the line, yet they answer with the typical *Hello* or *Hi, Mama!* and their listening ear is greeted with my raucous "GobbleGobbleGobble" that goes on and on and on. And so the laughter and conversation begin.

Two events made a recent Thanksgiving especially

memorable. First, I spent the week prior to the actual holiday with my daughter Anna and grandson Marshall. Since moving to the farm, I try to see them for a weekend every other month, but spending a whole week was a real treat. There's nothing like exploring and shopping, making an ooey-gooey pizza, and watching a movie together as a family.

The second out-of-the-ordinary event occurred the day before Thanksgiving. I was framing artwork at my part-time job in town, while visions of pumpkin pie danced in my head. My plan was to make the pie right after work. Of course I couldn't dive right into pie preparation as soon as I walked in the door. Sections of the newspaper lying helter-skelter atop the table were patiently waiting to be straightened and put away. Next, the morning's breakfast dishes, still piled in the sink, started calling my name. I had just washed and rinsed the last of them when our old-fashioned wall phone jangled. Drying my hands, I picked up the receiver. "Hello?"

"GobbleGobbleGobble." It was my daughter Katie, calling from New York. She turned the tables on me! When we finally stopped laughing, I settled into a comfy chair and we talked about everything and nothing for a fleeting forty-five minutes.

The pie had to wait until after supper, another round of dishes, and evening chores. Was I upset and bent out of shape that things hadn't come together according to my plan? No way! That evening I was still singing the praises of my sweet family as I gathered the ingredients for the pie. My parents and siblings, my aunts and uncles and cousins, and my own offspring, though not close in physical location, are clutched tightly in my heart. It's effortless to give thanks for them all, each and every day. An "interruption" from any of them is always a celebration.

This year's Thanksgiving Day gathering was at Beth and Steve's home. We were running just a little late, and as Weldon backed down the driveway he said, "I need to stop and put silage out for the cows. It will only take a minute." *Grrrr.* Grrrr? This is supposed to be Happy GobbleGobbleGobble Day. Ooops! I promptly gave thanks that all the crud around the silo was dry and hard-packed so he didn't get back in the car with you-know-what caked on the bottom of his shoes.

Thus we arrived, in our usual fashion, just a little late. (Can you hear my frustration in the phrase "just a little late"? Yes, I was still *grrrr*-ing.) After hugs all around and some friendly family chatter, everyone was ready to chow down. But first we formed a circle, held hands, and, one by one, said what we were thankful for. "I'm thankful for my teeth" (and, no, I'm not going to tell you that story). "I'm thankful for my children and my wife." "I'm thankful that I've lived another year." "I'm so thankful for an easy pregnancy." Some named a few things, some got teary-eyed, but everyone included thanks and praise to God for family.

This farm family has been an incredible blessing to me. I've said it before and I'll say it again: "I don't know if I could have survived life on the farm if it weren't for Weldon's amazing family." It's not easy for me to appreciate all things farm-related, with all the frustrations and muddle, but there's nothing easier than thanking God for the Keiger family and the way they enrich my life on a daily basis.

Thanksgiving Day had arrived like every other day and left us with overly stuffed hearts and tummies. Aah, such contentment. Surely giving of thanks cannot happen just once a year. Hundreds of Bible verses tell us to be thankful, and medical studies have proved that gratitude increases our health and sense of well-being. Give thanks to God. Give thanks for everything that comes your way. Rejoice right in the middle of the yuck and the setbacks. Be grateful to and for the people around you. On and on, over and over again.

A.A. Milne[38] wrote: "Piglet noticed that even though he had a very small heart, it could hold a rather large amount of gratitude." Gratitude begets gratitude. Go ahead and try it. Notice one thing and give thanks for that one thing. Find another something and be grateful. Family, friends, strangers; flowers, clouds, sunsets; surprises, disappointments, setbacks. Go through a whole day and see how many times you can say *thank you*. The act of expressing appreciation gets easier and easier. Our grateful words reach God's ears and, at the same time, lighten and brighten our faces.

"What a glorious day. Let's take a hike around Pilot Mountain."

"Yay! These sweet rolls are buy-one-get-one free."

"It's raining. My flowers are singing."

Gratitude is contagious. Speaking your thanks aloud may garner goofy looks but, more likely, the hearer will find his heart echoing the same sentiment and will respond in like manner.

Read Melody Beattie's quote again: "Gratitude unlocks the fullness of life. It turns what we have into enough, and more. It turns denial into acceptance, chaos to order, confusion to clarity. It can turn a meal into a feast, a house into a home, a stranger into a friend. Gratitude makes sense of our past, brings peace for today, and creates a vision for tomorrow."

Gratitude. I've used it like a topical ointment, but I'm learning it's more like a miracle drug...no prescription needed.

31

CAN'T RETIRE FROM CRAP

Being happy doesn't mean that everything is perfect. It means
that you've decided to look beyond the imperfections.

~Anonymous

Although I no longer help milk cows, morning and evening still find me out feeding cats and calves. Weldon continues with all the dairy farm chores and Pat has perfected her role as SuperWoman, helping with almost everything except the actual milking. When a need arises, I'm still called upon to lend a helping hand, and I'm glad to do it.

Take this evening. I had just fed the cats, and a few snowflakes were silently tumbling to the ground as I walked to the milk barn. I helped Pat load the little red wagon with two five-gallon pails of hot water, each holding two or three bottles of milk for the calves. Pat pulled the wagon, and I pushed with one hand while we carefully made our way up the soggy, slippery incline. In my other hand I carried a small bucket that held two more milk bottles.

While waiting for Weldon outside the calf pen, there was a lot of commotion in the lounging barn. "Let me see what's going on in there," Pat said. A few moments later, I followed. She was on the far side of the barn, waving her arms and yelling at the cows. "Get up! Get away from there! No! Get back!" Sidling up to her, I saw the cows escaping through a gate that was hanging at a precarious angle.

"Go tell Weldon that the cows are getting out!"

Back to the milk parlor I scurry. "The cows are getting out at that back gate over there! Come on!"

Minutes later, Weldon came running, flashlight in hand. The three of us propped the fence panels up by leaning one against another. "I'll go get the four-wheeler and round up the girls," he said, handing his light to Pat. She then passed it over to me, saying she was going to get her own, which gave a better light.

Quick as a wink, Weldon came careening up on the four-wheeler, herding five or six cows ahead of him. They were coming straight to the gates we had just propped up...but where was Pat? What was I supposed to do now?

I knew I couldn't stand in front of the wobbly barrier we had made, so I stepped as far to one side as I could. Sure enough, here came the girls. CRASH go the metal gates. "Be careful girls. Careful. Slowly now." I could picture one of them breaking a leg as they traversed the downed panels, but one by one they hip-hopped their way through and we herded them into the holding pen where they would wait until the other milk cows were brought in.

Pat was back with her flashlight, her pockets stuffed with baling twine (the farmer's go-to solution for almost every unexpected problem). We held the fence panels in place while Weldon secured them with the lengths of twine.

He hopped onto the four-wheeler to round up the rest of the renegades who were lollygagging in the field in front of the milk barn. Pat stood in the middle of the main road and I took my position on the road that runs through the barnyard. We would do our best to direct the cows through the open gate.

Then, what to our wondering eyes should appear but Nurse Nora (our biggest white cow) bounding OUT through the gate we had just opened. And I do mean bounding. She kicked up her heels, twisting and turning in midair like a bucking bronco. There was no containing her or getting her to turn around, so Pat and I just erupted in silly laughter.

Nurse Nora quickly encountered her cohorts who were being chased by a crazy farmer atop a roaring vehicle. Pat and I did our best big-arm waves and directed them in through the open gate. All of them except Nurse Nora, of course. She was just crazy! She continued down past the hay barn, but Weldon was hot on her heels. Within a few moments she was prancing back toward the open gate and, with a few more lively kicks thrown in for good measure, she and the others were safely secured in the holding pen. Pat and I were still chuckling.

"Okay, let's feed the calves," Weldon said. No complaining. No swearing. What a guy! We began with the youngest, but there were only three where there should have been four. One had escaped into the next pen where the five older ones were kept. Without batting an eye, Weldon started to feed two of the youngsters and I gave a bottle to the third.

Unfortunately, the rowdies in the next pen wanted to be fed NOW. They were all straining against the wooden pallets that separate the two areas. Sure enough, one broke through the slats. I simply grabbed another bottle and, in no time flat, the first four were fed.

We exchanged the empty bottles for five full bottles and moved to the upper stall. The older calves sucked greedily, and a couple of the just-fed younger ones found their way through the broken pallet and started nuzzling and butting, hoping to get a little more milk. What a zoo! If this sounds awfully confusing, you've got the picture.

Pat tied the gates and pallets together to keep the rascals in place for the evening. Weldon headed to the milk parlor to start the milking. In my heart of hearts, I was ready to go home, but instead I loaded the wagon with the empty buckets and bottles and pulled it back to the milk barn.

I washed the bottles, the nipples and rings, the dirty buckets, and then went back outside to rinse out the wagon. It didn't take long, and it felt good to know there were fewer tasks left for Pat to do on this goofy, messed-up evening.

When I finished in the milk parlor, I petted the four kittens that were piled on top of a cardboard barrel and called to Weldon as I walked out the door, "Hope milking goes well."

Passing by the hay barn, I saw Pat pitching hay into the calf pens. I petted a few cats and yoohooed, "Don't work too hard. Thanks for all you do." I waved and continued on my way.

At the big shed, I bent down with my final benediction. "Goodnight, kitties. Stay safe. Keep warm." I picked up the cat food bowl, crossed the road, and walked up the sidewalk to the house.

I hope you noticed I didn't pout and wallow tonight. I've grown, I'm not exhausted, and life goes on. Also, I was thinking, "When I get to the house, I'm going to write about this crap!" And that's just what I did.

32

IN CONCLUSION

The great thing, if one can, is to stop regarding all the unpleasant things as interruptions of one's 'own,' or 'real' life. The truth is of course that what one calls the interruptions are precisely one's real life—the life God is sending one day by day.

~C.S. Lewis[39]

And there you have it. Crap happens at your house, too, doesn't it?

Although this book is full of pitiful stories about the daily frustrations I encounter on the dairy farm, I hope you won't turn away with a sigh of depression. Yes, stuff and nonsense happens, but so does joy. Such is life.

As I mentioned in the first chapter, it's all about our attitude, the focus of our thoughts and hearts. "I can't believe all this crap!" Wallow, wallow, wallow. "What a gorgeous morning!" Dance, dance, dance. We have choices to make all day long. Inspect your inner cogitations, check your heart. What's growing there? If it's the oh-woe-is-me weed, pull it up by the roots. Search for the seeds of hidden beauty. Cultivate contentment. Joy is often staring us in the face; other times we have to look more closely, maybe even getting out the magnifying glass. When you find that smile, don't let it go. What does that song say? Accentuate the positive!

It's been over a year since I retired from milking cows. I just mixed up a blueberry slump and put it in the oven. I was smiling as I came back to my computer. Writing, baking, being a homebody—it's what I do. Participating in farm duties was good and important and eye-opening. At times it felt like it was more than my heart, mind, and body could handle, but it added a new dimension to who I am.

After ten years on the farm, I've learned all the lessons and my life is now perfect. Ha! Not quite. Life is a struggle and always will be. Since the difficulties won't end until the end, I'll take one day at a time, one hurdle at a time, one step at a time. If I mess up today, I'll try to do better tomorrow. And, if I mess up again tomorrow, I'm still secure in the love of God.

Absolutely nothing you or I do will make God love us more (or less) than he already does. He's crazy wild about me and he's not holding my mistakes or my wallowing against me. He's crazy wild about you, too. If you take nothing else away from this book, I hope you grab onto this one fact, because it will change your life: God loves you with an everlasting love…and there's nothing you can do to negate that truth.

There are many Bible verses that talk about the end or the conclusion of a matter, but Philippians 4:8 has always been one of my favorites: "And now, dear brothers and sisters, one final thing. Fix your thoughts on what is true, and honorable, and right, and pure, and lovely, and admirable. Think about things that are excellent and worthy of praise."

This is wonderful advice that can be difficult to remember, especially when I'm in the middle of yuck. I printed this verse on a decorative piece of paper and hung it in my bathroom, right next to the mirror. Every morning I smile at myself in the mirror as I read the words, vowing to put them into practice throughout the day.

Knowing the truth isn't the same as living the truth. I miss the mark many times, but my heart's desire is to live the way I believe. The lessons and advice I've shared in this book are just that—lessons and advice. I study, I pray, I purpose to do the right thing, but it doesn't always happen as neat and clean as it might sound. Until God makes a bit of wisdom clear and real to my heart, for my specific situation, all the books and the best advice from the sages of the world can't make a lasting change in my attitude. Even reading the words of the Bible aren't enough. God has to make it *real* to me, *for* me.

You've probably noticed that I'm not a huge fan of farm life. However, beauty and a surprising serenity sneak into my heart every now and then. While washing dishes this morning, I looked out the kitchen window and saw Weldon down in the sun-dappled field, mowing hay. This is the life he loves, the only life he has ever known. I walked to the milk parlor to get a jug of milk and felt admiration and joy at seeing the huge, round bales of hay piled along the road. Weldon did this! This is what he does…and he does it well.

My book is ending, but hassles and troubles never end. Icky stuff still happens, and wallowing is always an option. With God's help, let's keep walking … always watching out for the crap.

33

POSTSCRIPT

Wise words satisfy like a good meal;
the right words bring satisfaction.

~Proverbs 18:20

I have one final story to tell, as nourishing and satisfying as a good meal.

• • •

One of my earliest childhood memories is of sitting on the living room floor in front of the boxy black and white television set. My brothers are around me, and Ma and Pa sit behind us on the sagging couch. All eyes are fixed on the screen and our ears are listening to Billy Graham as he speaks to a huge crowd ... and to us.

If you've ever seen one of his crusades, you know they always ended the same way. George Beverly Shea would sing "Just As I Am"[40] after Mr. Graham made his closing remarks, inviting those who wanted to "ask Jesus into your heart" to come forward for prayer. "You who are watching this telecast from the comfort of your home can ask Jesus to come into your heart right where you are, just as you are."

I did that. Every time. The words always moved me in an inexplicable way.

There's nothing wrong with the picture of inviting Jesus into your heart, but many years later it became clear to me that Jesus didn't "just" want to live in my heart—he wanted my whole life. As the old hymn says, "All to Jesus I surrender, All to Him I freely give; I will ever love and trust Him, In His presence daily live."[41] In 1972, to the best of my ability, I gave my life (all of it) to Jesus. He made me, so I belonged to him; he wasn't just tucked away in my heart, but I was tucked away in his.

Regardless of the stories and advice I've shared in this book describing how I overcame (and continue to overcome) problems on the farm and in my life in general, all my self-help, best intentions, and strength come from my Father God and his son, Jesus.

Your life can be made new with a simple prayer: "Lord, I need you. I come to you. I give my life into your keeping. Live your life through me. Thank you."

Start reading the Bible. Find a contemporary version that is easy to understand. Talk to God on a daily basis, right in the middle of whatever you're doing. You'll see changes in the way you think, respond, and act. The best change is God's amazing peace that wraps you up and keeps you safe. When crap happens (and it will), look for God and accept his help.

I look forward to seeing you in the "life romantic" on the other side.

ACKNOWLEDGMENTS

The thought of writing a book about life on the farm started dancing around in my head almost ten years ago. In 2012, I finally determined to make the thought a reality. It has been a long, discouraging, hilarious adventure.

My first thanks go to Sue Babcock, Perry McDaid, Rick Taubold, and Lyn Gerry at silverpenwriters.org. In late 2012 and early 2013, I posted a few rough chapters on the site, and you gave me positive feedback, clear suggestions, and lots of encouragement.

In my usual fashion, I let things fall by the wayside. Then, in October of 2013, I heard about National Novel Writing Month. At nanowrimo.org I learned it was acceptable to write a memoir or whatever one wanted to write. The goal: 50,000 words in 30 days, but I couldn't use what I had already written. I was pumped...and I was successful. It was a mess, but it was 50,278 words that I could whip into shape at a later date.

I spent 2013 doing a little rewriting and editing, but it was easy to let it slide. When NaNoWriMo 2014 came around, I discovered I could use the month to edit 50,000 words instead of writing something new. And that's just what I did. Thank you, NaNoWriMo. I couldn't have done it without you.

There aren't enough words to express my heartfelt appreciation to the entire Keiger family. Your constant love, acceptance, and encouragement keep me going. Hugs all around.

My daughter Anna was the first to read the early chapters of this book. Thank you for your honest, helpful, and sometimes eye-opening comments and suggestions.

My daughter Katie has been my technical guru through the publishing process and has answered countless questions and given me courage to see this thing through to the end. Kudos to you.

I extend special thanks to Ralph and Dorothy Bressler, Rhoda Saatela, and Pat Keiger for reading the finished manuscript. I sincerely appreciate the time you took to give me your honest feedback.

Thank you, Viga Boland, for publishing the Introduction to my book in *Memoirabilia - The Magazine for Memoir Writers* (June/July 2015). You made me believe I could be an author.

And finally, if you've encouraged me along the way, if you've chuckled over any of my stories or commiserated with me about the yuck of life on a working farm…Thank You!

● ● ●

P.S. I will frolic and kick up my heels like Nurse Nora if you would take the time to go to Amazon.com and review *Crap Happens…Wallowing Is Optional.*

SOURCES

1   The North American Review *"What Paul Bourget Thinks of Us"*. 1895

2   Snowbird Gravy and Dishpan Pie. (Page 12) Ginns, Patsy Moore. The University of North Carolina Press. 1982

3   Quoted in *A Year of Beautiful Thoughts* (1902) by Jeanie Ashley Bates Greenough

4   Unsourced quote

5   Letter to John Clellon Holmes (Jun 24, 1949), published in *The Beat Vision: A Primary Sourcebook* (1987) edited by Arthur Knight and Kit Knight

6   Walking with God in Every Season: Ecclesiastes/Song of Solomon/Lamentations- Kay Arthur, Pete De Lacy Harvest House Publishers (Mar 1, 2010)

7   http://quoteswise.com

8   http://thinkexist.com Perhaps from her self-published book Blackberry Winter (no date)

9   My Utmost for His Highest, The Golden Book of Oswald Chambers, Barbour Publishing, Inc. 1994

10 Open My Eyes That I May See. Clara H. Scott (1895)

11 Quoted in The Entrepreneurial Ben Franklin, by James Charles Bouffard, published by Lynn Paulo Foundation (Feb 18, 2009)

12 No Ajahn Chah - Reflections, Compiled & Edited by Dhamma Garden https://www.ajahnchah.org/pdf/no_ajahn_chah.pdf

13 Words and music by Malvina Reynolds; copyright 1962 Schroder Music company, renewed 1990

14 The Complete Works of William Shakespeare, edited by W.G. Clark and W. Aldis Wright. Nelson Doubleday, Inc. Book Club Edition

15 No Man Is an Island. Mariner Books (Oct 28, 2002)

16 https://en.wikipedia.org/wiki/Trucker_hat

17 Blackthink: My Life as Black Man and White Man. By Jesse Owens. Published by William Morrow; 1st edition (Jun 1970)

18 The World According to Mister Rogers, by Fred Rogers. Published by Hachette Books (Oct 8, 2003)

19 Mere Christianity, by C.S, Lewis. Granite Publishers, Inc (Jan 1, 2006)

20 The Beverly Hillbillies. TV Series 1962-1971 Creator: Paul Henning

21 Reluctant Xtian Blog, Timothy Brown. https://reluctantxtian.wordpress.com/2014/01/31/what-we-lose-when-we-exorcise-mystery-from-faith/ (accessed Jan 31, 2014)

22 Stick a Geranium in Your Hat and Be Happy, by Barbara Johnson. Word Publishing, 1990

23 Poems of Power, by Ella Wheeler Wilcox . Chicago : W. B. Conkey, 1902

24 Fictional character on The Andy Griffith Show (1960-1968), played by Don Knotts

25 Unsourced quote

26 These Are the Gifts I'd Like to Give You: A Sourcebook of Joy and Encouragement. Douglas Pagels, editor. Published by Blue Mountain Arts (Sep 1999)

27 Overcoming Boredom. [PDF] http://www.texsource.com/bible/Boredom.pdf (page 6, accessed Sep 20, 2015)

28 The New York Times on the Web. Erikson, in His Own Old Age, Expands His View of Life. By Daniel Goleman. https://www.nytimes.com/books/99/08/22/specials/erikson-old.html (accessed Sep 26, 2015)

29 Bette Davis Biography on IMDb. http://www.imdb.com/name/nm0000012/bio

30 Enormous Smallness: A Story of E. E. Cummings by Matthew Burgess. Published by Enchanted Lion Books (Apr 7, 2015)

31 Stan Freberg parody of *Dragnet*. Misattributed to Joe Friday. https://en.wikipedia.org/wiki/Joe_Friday

32 Letters to a Young Poet. By Rainer Maria Rilke. Translated by M.D. Herter Norton. Published by W. W. Norton & Company; Revised edition (Aug 1, 1993)

33 The Accidental Missionary blog. https://theaccidentalmissionary.wordpress.com/2015/02/25/busy-is-a-sickness/ (accessed Feb 28, 2015)

34 The Ranch. This Day's Thought, Nov 12, 2013. http://theranch.org/2013/11/12/ray-pritchard-gods-mercies-come-day-by-day/

35 From Plato's account of the trial of Socrates, as noted in Wikiquote. https://en.wikiquote.org/wiki/Socrates

36 Blessings, by Laura Mixon Story. Published by Lyrics © Universal Music Publishing Group

37 Quoted in A Day in My Quote Book blog. http://adayinmyquotebook.com/2013/05/06/5613-gratitude-unlocks-the-fullness-of-life/

38 The Complete Tales of Winnie-the-Pooh, by A.A. Milne, illustrated by Ernest H. Shephard. Published by Dutton Books for Young Readers; 1st Thus. edition (Oct 1, 1996)

39 from a letter to Arthur Greeves, Dec 20, 1943

40 Charlotte Elliott. 1835. Copyright: Public Domain

41 I Surrender All by Judson W. Van DeVenter. 1896. Copyright: Public Domain